THE
GIFT
OF
RUMI

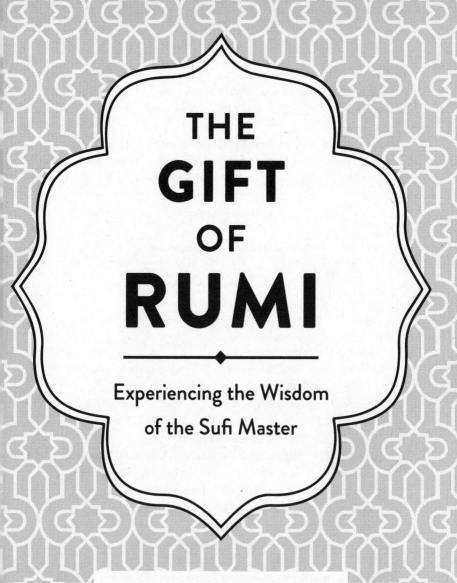

THE
GIFT
OF
RUMI

◆

Experiencing the Wisdom
of the Sufi Master

EMILY JANE O'DELL

ST. MARTIN'S
ESSENTIALS
NEW YORK

First published in the United States by St. Martin's Essentials, an imprint
of St. Martin's Publishing Group

www.stmartins.com

Designed by Steven Seighman

Title page shapes and vectors by Vecteezy

Library of Congress Cataloging-in-Publication Data

Names: O'Dell, Emily Jane, author.
Title: The gift of Rumi : experiencing the wisdom of the Sufi master /
   Emily Jane O'Dell.
Description: First edition. | New York : St. Martin's Essentials, 2022.
Identifiers: LCCN 2022012556 | ISBN 9781250261373 (trade
   paperback) | ISBN 9781250261380 (ebook)
Subjects: LCSH: Jalāl al-Dīn Rūmī, Maulana, 1207-1273—Criticism
   and interpretation. | Islam in literature | Mysticism in literature. |
   Spirituality in literature. | LCGFT: Literary criticism.
Classification: LCC PK6482 .O34 2022 | DDC 891/.5511—dc23/
   eng/20220506
LC record available at https://lccn.loc.gov/2022012556

Our books may be purchased in bulk for promotional, educational, or
business use. Please contact your local bookseller or the Macmillan Corporate
and Premium Sales Department at 1-800-221-7945, extension 5442, or by
email at MacmillanSpecialMarkets@macmillan.com.

First Edition: 2022

10 9 8 7 6 5 4 3 2 1

This book is dedicated to your yearning heart . . .

CONTENTS

INTRODUCTION

◆

Mawlana Jalal al-Din Muhammad Balkhi (1207–1273), more commonly known in the West as Rumi, was a brilliant poet and celebrated mystic from the thirteenth century, whose lyrical and ecstatic articulations of divine love have touched and inspired hearts around the world since medieval times until the present day. Born in Central Asia, Rumi migrated west with his parents as a boy to Anatolia during a period of extreme regional instability and uncertainty due to the ongoing Mongol invasions and local power struggles. Though Rumi has been lauded as a "best-selling poet" in America for decades and many have heard of his message of love, the mystical meanings and spiritual contexts of his poems have been crying out for more attention.

Many people today are hungry for spiritual nourishment and in search of something greater than themselves. The usual uncertainties and anxieties of life have been compounded by the recent tumult of political events and the carnage of an ongoing global pandemic. Life as we knew it has been upended. Caught between the crushing waves of rising intolerance and mass death, many souls across the world are seeking to soothe their sorrow, anger, and alienation in this unjust world that glorifies materialism and worships wealth above all else. Rumi, whose own day was marked by violent chaos and mass death, offers us a portal out of our despair. He invites us to: "Rise from the plague of hypocrisy and deprivation, and enter the world of life and self-subsistence." Through his celebrated verse, Rumi gently guides us to become free from our attachments to the material realm and our own "self" through reflection, devotion, and the overpowering force of love. A touch of insanity doesn't hurt, either!

In his poetry, Rumi frequently refers to Islamic mysticism, or Sufism, as "the way" or "the path" that leads away from worldliness toward the divine realm. Sufism is the road of love that a yearning heart takes in its journey toward truth. It is a mystic path tread by spiritual wayfarers with polished hearts and perfected virtue who strive in every moment—with each breath—to experience divine love. Rumi does not only use the words "Sufi" and "dervish" for Muslim mystics—he also calls them the dear ones, the poor ones, the lovers, the people of purity, the friends, the wanderers, the freed ones, the aware ones, the knowers of God, the people of the heart, and those who are truly existent. A mystic master himself, Rumi's exemplary spiritual life and visionary poetry exude the compassionate spirit of religious tolerance, celebrate the healing power of the creative arts, and unveil the heights of spiritual ecstasy and transcendence. To uncover the deeper meanings of Rumi's poetry, this book contextualizes his exalted verses in the essentials of Islamic mysticism.

What is the gift of Rumi? The gift of Rumi is, first and foremost, love. Rumi was a mystic preacher of love who professed the healing and transformative power of love. He was a poetic master who beautifully captured the sweet pain of the heart's yearning for greater intimacy with the divine. At the core of Rumi's mystical poetry is the "religion of love," which transcends all religions. As Rumi wrote: "The religion of love is separate from all religions. For lovers, the only creed and doctrine is God." A devout Muslim, Rumi refers to God in his poetry as "the beloved"—the source of love itself. Through his majestic verses of ecstasy and longing, Rumi invites us into the religion of the heart and guides us to our own loving inner essence. His playful and profound articulation of the soul's journey back to its pure nature and loving source is a gift to all humanity.

Rumi's given name was Muhammad. The honorific, Jalal al-Din, given to him by his father, means "Splendor of the Faith." Arabic, Persian, and Turkish speakers in the past and present do not refer to him as "Rumi." Rather, they call him "Mawlana" or "Mevlana," which means "Our Master" or "Our Teacher." The moniker "Rumi" means "The One from Rum," with "Rum" referring to Byzantium, the eastern half of the Roman Empire, which included the territory of modern-day Turkey, where Rumi lived for most of his life. The nickname "Rumi" gained currency in the 1920s and 1930s, as a result of its usage and propagation by western Orientalists. Rumi is buried in Konya, which during his life was the capital of the Seljuk Sultanate of Rum in south-central Turkey.

As Rumi wrote mainly in Persian, his poetry has been recited through the centuries by Persian speakers in what is modern-day Iran, Afghanistan, Tajikistan, and Uzbekistan, as well as the Indo-Pakistan subcontinent. All along the Silk Road, Muslims for centuries have sung his poems in many different languages as lyrics for their traditional music genres and forms—such as *qawwali* in India and Pakistan and *shashmaqam* in Central Asia. Rumi's poetry still plays a central function in the lives of millions of Muslims around the world. In fact, in his poems he references geographies far and wide with allusions to Egypt, Yemen, Iran, Turkey, Uzbekistan, Kazakhstan, China, Syria, Iraq, India, Oman, and beyond. Rumi's poetry, in the past and present, has influenced and inspired writers in many languages, such as Arabic, Persian, Urdu, Hindi, Pashto, Turkish, Tamil, Gujarati, and Chinese. Rumi also knew Arabic, and he wrote hundreds of poems in Arabic, too.

Rumi was a revered Muslim scholar, jurist, and mystic. As a Muslim, he observed the five pillars of Islam—the profession of faith, the daily prayers, the giving of charity, the fasting of Ramadan, and the pilgrimage to Mecca. He was a Sunni Muslim who practiced Islamic mysticism, and he followed the Hanafi school of Islamic jurisprudence. His father, Baha al-Din Walad, was also a respected Muslim preacher, theologian, and scholar of the Qur'an. In the words of Rumi's spiritual master, Shams of Tabriz, the Qur'an is the "Book of Love." Rumi draws frequently from the Qur'an in his poetic masterpiece, *The Masnavi*, which explores the spiritual journey of a soul returning to its source through a variety of tales and Quranic allusions. However, in many popular English translations of Rumi's verse, a significant portion of Islamic references have been left out.

Some of the selections in this book come from *The Masnavi*, which Rumi described as "the roots of the roots of the roots of religion" and "the explainer of the Qur'an." Many have called his six-volume masterpiece with over 25,000 verses the "Qur'an in the Persian language." Perhaps no other text apart from the Qur'an, the holy text of Islam, which was recited by the Prophet Muhammad in Mecca and Medina in the seventh century, has so influenced the lives of Muslims around the world as Rumi's *Masnavi*. As Rumi explains: "My Masnavi is the shop for unity—anything that you see except the 'One' is an idol." Rumi also wrote sermons and thousands of odes and quatrains, a number of which are also featured in these pages.

Rumi's verses of love and spiritual ecstasy have resonated with countless hearts around the world through translation, but his poetry in the original Persian is even more dazzling than most people realize. Many of Rumi's poems are so spiritually deep (the words and meanings can be translated in a multitude of ways) that native speakers of Persian can debate for hours, days, and even weeks about just one verse or even one word. A significant amount of Persian scholarship on Rumi is still not translated into English, and a large portion of his own oeuvre has not yet been translated into English.

Through the ages, poetry has been an essential element of Persian culture. In almost every Persian home today, you can find the poetry of Rumi and other celebrated Persian poets, such as Ferdowsi, Sana'i, Abu Hamid bin Abu Bakr Ibrahim (Attar), Sa'di, Hafez, and Abu Sa'id Abi'l-Khayr. Every time I have visited the tomb of Rumi in Turkey and the mausoleums of Hafez and Sa'di in Shiraz in the Islamic Republic of Iran, I have been touched and inspired by the devotion of the countless hearts gathered around the tombs of these medieval poetic masters, clutching their immortal words in their hands and paying their respects in person. As one Iranian friend said to me, "My teachers are Omar Khayyam, Hafez, and Rumi. Omar Khayyam is my logic—there is nothing to this world. Hafez is my heart. He teaches me beyond love and compassion. Rumi is my destination. To become one! The 'one' is the self. To become one's true self."

In the Islamic Republic of Iran today, politicians frequently invoke these Persian poets for their domestic audience. The centrality of poetry in Persian culture is why President Obama, in one of his Persian New Year video messages, quoted from the famous Persian poet Sa'di: "There are those who insist that we be defined by our differences. But let us remember the words that were written by the poet Sa'di, so many years ago: 'The children of Adam are limbs to each other, having been created of one essence.'" These same words are engraved on the entrance of the United Nations in New York City.

Writers and travelers in the West have been captivated by Persian poetry for centuries. Dervishes appear in Western travel accounts and memoirs as early as the fifteenth century. Scholars believe that perhaps the earliest reference to Persian poetry in English is George Puttenham's inclusion of four anonymous "Oriental" poems translated from Persian in *The Arte of English Poesie* in 1589. In fact, Sa'di's masterpiece, *Gulistan*, was introduced to French, Latin, and German readers as early as the eighteenth century. Johann Wolfgang von Goethe drew inspiration from Hafez for his *West-Eastern Divan*, published in 1827, and Gertrude Bell (d. 1926), who infamously helped draw the borders of the modern Middle East, also published translations of Hafez. Persian poetry had a profound influence on romantic and transcendental poetry in America due to its universalist and humanist themes.

Some of the most celebrated early American writers drew inspiration from Sa'di's *Gulistan*, Hafez's *Divan*, Omar Khayyam's *Ruba'iyyat*, and Rumi's *Masnavi*—which were all accessible to Western audiences as early as the eighteenth century. American writers such as Ralph Waldo Emerson, Walt Whitman, Mark Twain, Herman Melville, Henry David Thoreau, and Henry Wadsworth Longfellow were influenced by these Persian masterpieces, and they put themselves in dialogue with these celebrated Persian poets. As Thoreau (d. 1862) wrote about the Persian poet Sa'di: "I know, for instance, that Saadi entertained once identically the same thought that I do, and thereafter I can find no essential difference between Saadi and myself. He is not Persian, he is not ancient, he is not strange to me." Post–Civil

War American poets were drawn to Persian poetry's themes of nature, suffering, and transcendence.

Ralph Waldo Emerson (d. 1882), who was first drawn to Persian poetry as a child, helped to popularize Persian poetry in America. Like Whitman and Thoreau, Emerson was drawn most to Sa'di, and he even wrote a poem titled "Saadi" in 1842 that used Sa'di as an alter ego. Emerson wrote, "He inspires in the reader a good hope. What a contrast between the cynical tone of Byron and the benevolent wisdom of Saadi!" Emerson translated hundreds of lines of Sa'di's Persian poetry into English from the German translation done by Friedrich Rückert (d. 1866).

Translations of Rumi's poetry into European languages emerged in the late eighteenth century. Rumi was translated into German by Friedrich Rückert, Friedrich Rosen (d. 1935), Georg Rosen (d. 1961), and Austrian scholar Joseph von Hammer-Purgstall (d. 1856), whose translations of passages from Rumi's *Masnavi* and *Divan-e Shams* directly inspired Goethe. Aflaki's thirteenth-century hagiographical account of Rumi was translated into French by Clément Huart (d. 1926). Reynold A. Nicholson published fifty Rumi poems in English in 1898, and soon after a groundbreaking translation of *The Masnavi*. Rumi's other twentieth-century translators in English have included Arthur J. Arberry, Annemarie Schimmel, Eva de Vitray-Meyerovitch, William Chittick, Franklin D. Lewis, Jawid Mojaddedi, and others.

Though references to Rumi had been made in English by transcendentalists, who were aware of his poetry through the German translations of Hammer-Purgstall and F. A. G. Tholuck, and in the early twentieth century by the followers of the Indian Sufi master Hazrat Inayat Khan (d. 1927), founder of the Sufi Order of the West, the poetry of Rumi did not vault to mass popularity until after Robert Bly gave a copy of Arberry's translations to Coleman Barks in the 1970s. Because Barks was not familiar with Persian or the Qur'an, his collections are not necessarily accurate representations of Rumi's own words and ideas. However, Barks's popular translations did bring the figure of Rumi to millions in the West who were drawn to Barks's free-verse modern idiomatic reimaginings of Rumi's verse. In fact, one of my Iranian colleagues recently told me that Barks's freewheeling translations helped "unlock" the original for him and inspired him to return to reading Rumi in Persian. Many, however, have been much more critical of Barks and other popular translators of Rumi who have had no expertise or education in Persian or Islam.

While such translations have helped to spread awareness about Rumi and broadcast his message of universal love, they have often stripped his poems of their religious references and spiritual richness in order to make them ostensibly more acceptable and accessible to a mostly elite, white, and non-Muslim audience. In the Victorian era, cultural and religious references were cut from Rumi's poems, and this de-Islamization and Aryanization trend continued through the twentieth century. Thus, many published poems of Rumi have been robbed of their religious richness and mystical contexts to be more palatable to a Western audience. As a result, a number of Rumi's references to God, the prophets of Islam, and the tenets of Islam, as well as his bold moral proclamations and denunciations of wealth, have been disappeared.

This book seeks to restore and emphasize the Islamic and mystical contexts of Rumi's poetry. It is an attempt to meet Rumi on his own terms without distorting or mischaracterizing his words and message. It includes accessible spiritual commentary to help the reader excavate the deeper mystical meanings and allusions in his poems. This book does not mask Rumi's identity as a Muslim, but instead aims to highlight the Islamic references in his verses to honor the pious and humble heart of this medieval Muslim mystic whose poetry is deeply spiritual in its content and humanist in its message—a message that still resonates today around the world in Muslim and non-Muslim hearts alike.

I have written this book in the genre of a medieval dervish manual to give a comprehensive introduction to Rumi's poetry, life, and legacy that is in keeping with a popular literary style of dervish instruction and Sufi ethos in Rumi's day. Medieval dervish manuals tended to have sections on love, travel, retreat, spiritual whirling, virtuous conduct, silence, contentment, discipleship, spiritual companionship, renunciatory piety, trust in God, and attitudes toward hardship. They instructed spiritual seekers on how to tame the ego, accept the ephemerality of the world, and purify the heart. The chapters in this book similarly highlight the most important aspects of mystic practice in Rumi's day. Scattered biographical details explain the formation of Rumi's worldview, and references to the religious discourse, intellectual trends, and philosophical debates of Rumi's day contextualize his spiritual vision.

The gift of Rumi is not just found in his poetic verses. The gift of Rumi lives on today in the mystic Muslims of the Mevlevi Order, who are stewards of his memory and strive to embody the noble virtues, compassionate nature, and loving essence that Rumi captures and celebrates in his poetry. To share with you how the mystic lineage and embodied legacies of Rumi's gift are lived and transmitted, I have included some moments from my forty-day retreat in Turkey with a Mevlevi master and his whirling dervishes. Through a bizarre set of circumstances, including mystical dreams that bestowed upon me the name Zemzem (an alternative spelling of Zamzam, the name of the holy well at Mecca), I found myself living in seclusion in one of the most religiously conservative corners of Istanbul with a Sufi shaykh and his disciples, where I was instructed in Rumi's message, taught how to whirl like a dervish, and guided in proper moral and virtuous dervish conduct.

Many years ago, hungry to read Rumi in the original Persian, I devoted myself to studying Persian at Brown University, Harvard University, and the American Institute of Iranian Studies in Tajikistan to experience Rumi in his own words. In the pages that follow, I have translated his poetry word for word, without consideration of rhyme or poetic style, to give you, the reader, the most literal version of his poetry in American English that I could render. The field of translation is vast, and obviously any translation is incapable of capturing the original. This book is not an attempt to be the "best" translation of Rumi's words, by any means. It does not attempt to replicate the rhyme in his poetry or poetically capture the essence of each line. Rather, it is an attempt to offer a sample of his verses with as much of a word-to-word correspondence with English as possible to let Rumi speak for himself.

As the third-person singular pronoun in Persian is not gendered (he/she), I have alternated how I translate the gender-neutral pronoun and thus tried to liberate Rumi's poems from masculine exclusionism. Rumi often uses the first-person plural ("we are"), which, like other translators, I have occasionally translated as the first-person singular ("I am"). I have inserted words only when absolutely necessary to convey the full meaning or context of a verse, and have added line breaks to aid reading his verses in English. I have given the selections simple titles for easy reference.

Rumi's poems on "love" have received the most attention in the West due to misinterpretations of them as romantic or sensual poetry, which has led to his poems that are focused on morality and proper ethical conduct being less frequently translated. A number of his poems have been deliberately mistranslated as being about sexual longing, when they are, in fact, about desiring closer spiritual intimacy with one's mystic guide or the divine. Much of the Rumi poetry that has been published for a general audience has focused on his blissful verses of love and affirmation, instead of his more critical, fiery, and confrontational verses that urge his readers to live more sincere, devotional, and unconventional lives. In such poems, Rumi encourages us to seek the eternal instead of the material, and he rebukes us for our heedlessness and misguided priorities. Now, perhaps more than ever, these neglected verses of Rumi speak to the cold materialism and lack of dynamic spirituality, morality, and selflessness that define our age.

There's a reason why people around the world like to stake a claim to the gift of Rumi. Afghans claim Rumi's family hailed from their territory, while Tajiks contend that Rumi was born in a river town within their present-day borders. Iranians point to Rumi's place in the Persian poetic canon to lay claim to his lineage, while Turks maintain that he spent the majority of his life in Anatolia and thus became one of their own. On the other side of the ocean, Americans frame him as the country's "bestselling poet." The gift of Rumi is, of course, for everyone, but belongs to no one—for how can anyone claim to own the ocean?

Finally, as Rumi noted, Sufis are the custodians of the secrets of the heart. These secrets, passed down from mystic master to disciple, unlock the heart and flood it with love from within. Due to the intricacy of this delicate spiritual art, dervish conversations are subtle and full of nuance founded on insider mystic knowledge. What is presented here is merely an introduction to Rumi's message and the invisible dimensions of Islamic mysticism. Mysticism, by its nature, cannot be known through words or learned knowledge—it can only be lived and experienced to be truly understood. Thus, these chapters are merely a taste of the gift of Rumi, and these words on the page but traces of a bleeding heart humbly trying to convey the indescribable and ineffable.

In the pages that follow, a map of love awaits you, but the treasure you must discover for yourself. May this collection of Rumi's verses serve as inspiration for your ailing heart—and a salve for your suffering soul. May your spirit find the blessed peace and heights of ecstasy it is seeking. And, finally, in the ruins of your heart and broken fragments of your soul, may you find the treasure.

ONENESS

Come closer, closer! How much more of this highway robbery?
Since you are me and I am you,
how much more of this
you being you and me being me?

With God, we are the light of truth and the glass.
How much more of this stubbornness with our own self?
How can luminosity flee from luminosity?

We are all one complete being.
Why are we seeing double like this?
Why should a rich person look at the poor with contempt?

Why should your right hand look at your left with disdain,
when they are both your hands—
whether they have done righteous deeds or vile.

We are all one substance, one mind, and one head—
but the curved heavens make us see double.

Move out from these five senses
and six directions toward oneness!
How much longer will you let
the juniper tree of unity
wither in two?

Hurry up! Leap from me-ness,
and mix with the all!
With your own self you are but a grain,
but mixed with everyone
you are a mine of jewels!

Whatever a male lion does,
the dog will behave the same as a dog.
Whatever the pure spirit does,
the body will act the same as a body.

Know that the spirit is one,
but the body has become numbered
a hundred thousand times—
just as almonds share
in being milky
when mixed together.

There are many languages in the world—
but all with one meaning.

*Water becomes one
when you break the jars.*

*The soul will send news to all
possessed of spiritual vision,
when you break
the heart
from words.*

WANDERING DERVISHES

◆

The world around Rumi was anything but peaceful. Rumi grew up and lived through an era of brutal war, political turmoil, and widespread migration across Central Asia and the Middle East. From childhood until his death, Rumi's life was shaped by the death and destruction wrought across the region by the ferocious Mongol armies. As an adult, Rumi was composing his poems about divine love and ecstatic bliss at the same time that the Mongols were invading and laying waste to Islam's most illustrious cities. Rumi himself lived in personal fear of the Mongol threat, and he even had nightmares about Mongol armies destroying Konya, where he lived most of his adult life. But since Rumi interpreted all events as manifestations of divine will, he believed that God himself, as the "Creator" of the Mongols as well as the Muslims, was the invisible force behind the destruction of the Muslim world.

I'm a Balkhi, I'm a Balkhi, I'm a Balkhi.
The world is in turmoil due to my bitterness.

Rumi was born on September 30, 1207. Tajiks maintain that he was born in the river town of Vakhsh, which today falls within the borders of modern-day Tajikistan, while Afghans maintain that Rumi was born in the city of Balkh in Afghanistan, since he was known as "al-Balkhi"—"The One from Balkh." At the time, however, the town of Vakhsh was under the administration of

Balkh and thus part of the Balkh region. On their migrations, Rumi's family identified as being from the greater Balkh region. Rumi's father, Baha al-Din Walad, was a preacher, religious teacher, and Sunni jurist whose legal orientation was the Hanafi school of jurisprudence, which was popular in Central Asia at the time and remains the most popular school of religious legal thought today in the region. Though Rumi's father wrote and taught about the esoteric spiritual dimensions of Islam, he did not identify as a dervish despite his mystic leanings.

> *Because you are in Balkh,*
> *journey on toward Baghdad, O father!*
> *So, with every breath, you will be farther away*
> *from Merv and Herat.*

Due to the Mongol invasions at the beginning of the thirteenth century, local political feuds, and professional rivalries, Rumi's father, Baha al-Din Walad, decided to take his family westward through territories that are now within the borders of modern-day Uzbekistan, Iran, Iraq, Syria, Turkey, and Saudi Arabia. The looming threats of violence and displacement made Rumi acutely aware of the transience, traumas, and uncertainties of life at the tender age of ten.

> *Wake up, O heart! The world is passing by!*
> *Life goes by like an asset you freely give away.*
> *In the house of the heart, don't sit asleep and unaware,*
> *as the caravan passes through the house of life.*

After traveling on the Silk Road through Balkh, Bukhara, Samarkand, Nishapur, Baghdad, Damascus, Aleppo, and Mecca, and meeting many spiritual communities and luminaries along the way, Rumi's family eventually put down roots in the Muslim minority community of Konya in modern-day Turkey, which was ruled over by the Seljuk Turks.

At that time, the eastern Roman Empire was known as "Rum" in Persian, which is how Rumi much later acquired the moniker "Rumi" for having lived in this Christian region dominated by Greeks and Armenians.

> *O you prisoners of the body:*
> *Go and see the sights of the soul!*
> *For in the end, the Messenger Muhammad said:*
> *"Seeing the sights is a blessing."*

Wandering with his family at such a formative age introduced Rumi to different spiritual traditions, sects, and practices. Despite the onslaught of the Mongol armies, Rumi lived in a golden age for Islamic philosophy and mysticism.

WANDERING HEART

> *O heart! One moment you're crazy,*
> *and the next you're lord of the court!*
>
> *Sometimes you attack Iran for plundering,*
> *and other times you go to its rival Turan*
> *and become the sheriff.*
>
> *Sometimes wandering in Isfahan, Hijaz, and Iraq,*
> *and other times serving as lead musician*
> *for the king of Khorasan—*
> *who is like the moon.*

In this poetry, Rumi frequently depicts himself as a reckless wanderer on the road—seeking after the pain of love and desperate for the mystical annihilation of selfhood. Death, of course, looms large in Rumi's poems because Muslim mystics stress the importance of dying to the self, or annihilating the ego and its desires, to advance on the mystical path of self-purification. To do so, a dervish must contemplate and accept the reality of her own actual death. As Rumi writes: "Know that this world, filled with sweets and bread, is like the open mouth of a crocodile." To taste sweet union with the eternal divine essence, we must first awaken to our mortality and finitude.

The secret of "Die before you die" is this:
that the riches come after dying.
Other than dying, no other knowledge
is suitable with God, O crafty one!

Sufis talk often of the secret of "Die before you die." This mystical death is an intentional rupture of one's attachment to ego, the material world, and identity. Dervishes try to free themselves from their attachments to the preoccupations of the ego to prepare themselves for their inevitable deaths and live the rest of their lives fully immersed in the loving presence of the divine. In the words of Rumi: "My life depends on my dying."

The flood water has surrounded the ruined
abode of life,
and the goblet of life is almost filled.
Be content, for the moment you blink your eyes,
the porter of time will carry your belongings
out of the house of life.

Rumi saw himself as a traveler—on both the physical and spiritual planes. As a child, he traveled through the illustrious cities of the Muslim world, and as an adult he was committed to exploring and sharing his inner spiritual journey.

> *In this era, I am a world traveler,*
> *leaving every city to its charms.*
> *Aimless like a boat in the ocean—*
> *every day anchoring in one place,*
> *and every night in another.*

For Rumi, a spiritual seeker was not attached to place, but was instead on an endless quest to journey outwardly for spiritual knowledge and inwardly to explore different mystical states. For a spiritual wayfarer, there is no need to participate in beautifying a city or a home, for a wandering dervish is not moored to one place or even her own life. Instead, such a mystic is happily lost at sea with no destination in mind. In the ocean of love, all a dervish needs is the sweet treasure in her own heart.

> *I carry sugar from Egypt to Byzantium,*
> *even though I have neither caravan driver nor caravan.*

Apart from fleeing the violence of the Mongol armies, medieval mystics like Rumi had a host of inner and outer motivations for wandering. As Muslims, dervishes had to make the obligatory religious pilgrimage to Mecca, and they also sought spiritual knowledge from different spiritual masters, religious institutions, and famed libraries, both near and far. Inwardly, travel was thought to help one discipline the soul, cultivate virtue, and retreat from the comforts of home into the secure house of the heart. Of course, wherever they wandered, dervishes carried the sweetness, or sugar, of love in their heart.

Beyond this tongue, our language is another.
Beyond heaven and hell, our abode is another.
Free hearts draw life from one another.
Our pure gem is from another mine.

For the dervish, the only true destination is union with the divine. Devotional travel, or spiritual wandering, was seen as a prime vehicle for spiritual awakening and transformation. In fact, some dervishes would roam through desolate desert lands in a state of spiritual bewilderment without any provisions, to test and prove their absolute dependence on the divine. Because humans tend to dislike change, leaving one's homeland to practice mystical wandering was a way to advance spiritually by combatting the attachments of the self to home, comfort, and habit.

It is a day of happiness—why should we suffer sorrow?
Today, we should drink wine from the cup of faithfulness!
How much sustenance will we eat from the palm of the baker,
and drink from the water carrier?
For a while, we should eat only from the hand of God.

Medieval dervish manuals even had sections called "Conduct in Travel," which included Sufi ethics for traveling, eating, and fasting while on the road, with additional advice on how to determine the proper direction and times for prayer while on a journey.

A Sufi is a child of the now, O friend.
Saying "tomorrow" is not a condition of the path.

In the years that followed Rumi's death, his son and followers of his message formed the Mevlevi Sufi Order to carry on Rumi's memory and honor him. Mevlevi lodges and whirling halls were eventually established throughout Asia Minor and the Levant to spread the spirit of Rumi's message. Hundreds of Mevlevi lodges appeared in corners of present-day Turkey, Iran, Ukraine, Hungary, Egypt, Palestine, Syria, Lebanon, Saudi Arabia, Bulgaria, and the Balkans. As a result, vestiges of the veneration of Rumi can still be found today throughout the Middle East, Africa, Central Asia, and Eastern Europe.

> *For how long will I whirl uselessly like dust?*
> *For how long will I wander on mountaintops and in caves?*
> *For how long will I whirl like a child around a lifeless doll?*
> *For once, I should whirl around a friend.*

In my more than two decades of traveling on the Silk Road, from preserving medieval Sufi shrines while living in a desert yurt in Turkmenistan to teaching and working with refugees in the Levant, I have encountered Rumi almost everywhere I have turned. In Egypt, where I spent many winters excavating tombs at the Pyramids of Giza, I attended a women's Sufi group in the Khan el-Khalili bazaar of Cairo next to a seventeenth-century Mevlevi lodge for whirling dervishes that incidentally bears a fitting spiritual inscription from a thirteenth-century medieval Arabic literary classic, *The Maqamat of al-Hariri*: "Poor is the son of Adam, oh, how poor! He relies upon the world, on that which is unreliable, and through his love for it, he is slaughtered thereby without a knife. He is addicted to it through his folly."

> *Though Pharaoh's deceitful tricks were three hundredfold,*
> *they all led to his humiliation and subjugation.*

While studying how to whirl like a dervish with a talented Egyptian teacher in Cairo, who spun so quickly that his body disappeared into a dizzying blur, I stepped inside the sacred turn to which Rumi gave his heart and soul—which lives on today in Egypt as a folk dance performance for tourists on Nile cruises and in the moonlit citadel of Cairo. The Nobel Prize–winning Egyptian writer Naguib Mahfouz once said of Sufism, "I can't help loving Sufism because it sounds so beautiful. It gives relief in the midst of the battle."

Jump in! For here is the fountain of life.
Whirl like the heavens, as long as that moon of yours whirls!
You have a soul—so whirl around the divine presence!
For this soul whirls by the whirling of that soul.

Reminders of Rumi are scattered around Central Asia, too. When I had the remarkable opportunity to help restore the mausoleum complex of the celebrated eleventh-century Persian mystic poet Yusuf Hamadani and tombs of the Companions of the Prophet Muhammad on the Silk Road in Turkmenistan, while excavating the medieval Islamic bazaar next to the tomb of Sultan Sanjar in Merv, I was reminded of Rumi's reverence in his poetry for that powerful Seljuk sultan and Rumi's own fear of the Mongols—who destroyed Merv in 1220. Hunting after long-abandoned caravanserais deep in the desert in Turkmenistan, I could imagine the long and arduous journeys Rumi's family took on the Silk Road through such physically challenging terrain.

Tonight, I am with a thousand hidden Sufis.
Like the soul, all of them are concealed and yet visible.
O gnostic and musician, go out and don't stop searching
until you find dancers of this exalted quality.

I was not fully aware of Rumi's connections to Tajikistan until I was studying Persian and Tajik in Dushanbe, where my teachers shared with me their pride in Rumi having been born within their present-day borders. They also taught us about the poetry of Rudaki, whose poems shaped how Rumi used and played with language.

While studying the *dutar,* or two-stringed lute, at the Tajik National Conservatory with Tajikistan's greatest *dutar* master, Sirojiddin Juraev, I listened enraptured while he sang lyrics from Rumi's poetry in the original Persian while performing songs from the *shashmaqam,* a Central Asian musical genre. In fact, some of the most renowned *shashmaqam* musicians were Bukharan Jews, whose mastery and dissemination of these songs with lyrics from the poetry of Rumi and Hafez helped keep the tradition alive. Now, whenever I find myself wandering through the legendary madrasas of Bukhara in neighboring Uzbekistan, I think of that musical tradition embedded in the poetry of Rumi and performed across borders and religions.

> *O Turk, why do you have curls like an Indian—*
> *with a Greek face, African beard, and a head*
>   *full of Chinese hair?*
> *Don't let your heart become lost in western China.*
> *I'm afraid that you're a Turk—so speak Turkish.*

From my time in Xinjiang (East Turkestan) in western China, I saw firsthand how traditional Uyghur music, specifically the Twelve Muqam suite, is woven through the culture there. Uyghur singers have traditionally performed the Twelve Muqam suite with lyrics from the Persian poetry of Rumi and Hafez. However, due to reforms in the mid-twentieth century, these Persian texts were replaced with canonical Chagatai Turkic poetry. Sadly, today, a number of celebrated Uyghur musicians and scholars of traditional Uyghur music in Xinjiang have been imprisoned in internment camps by the Chinese Communist Party.

> *In an instant, I am above the seven heavens.*
> *In an instant, I am in Syria and Iraq.*
> *In an instant, I am drowning in separation.*
> *In an instant, I cleverly uncover your secret.*

Remnants of centuries-old reverence for Rumi are embedded in the Levant, too. As the Whittlesey Chair of History and Archaeology at the American University of Beirut, I was very fortunate to be given a special private tour in Tripoli of a stunning Mevlevi Sufi Order lodge that was built in 1619 to carry on and share Rumi's message and memory. Damaged in a flood and neglected during the Lebanese Civil War, this Ottoman gem was restored with funding from Turkey in 2014, but it is not open to the public. I treasured being nestled in that historic oasis of peace and contemplation at a very tense time, when bombs were exploding regularly across Lebanon and the city of Tripoli itself was plagued with daily sectarian gun battles.

> *I became an intimate to the spiritual wayseekers.*
> *I became a companion to the inhabitants of Jerusalem.*

Historically, the shaykh of the Mevlevis in Tripoli appointed the shaykh of the Mevlevis in Jerusalem. When doing research on Sufism in Palestine, I noticed an old road in the heart of East Jerusalem that was marked with a sign that read: AL-MAWLAWIYYA ASCENT. Surely, I thought, this must be a clue that a Mevlevi Sufi lodge is nearby. For days I searched the bustling alleys of the Old City for a Sufi sign, and then, finally, one afternoon I noticed a locked green steel door under the arch of a stone-lined passageway with a sign hanging above it that said in Arabic: MEVLEVI MOSQUE. I knocked on the door and to my surprise, it opened. I was warmly ushered into the courtyard, where I was shown around this old Mevlevi Sufi lodge made of Jerusalem stone whose minaret was so tall it hardly fit into my camera frame. In fact, Palestinian Sufis performed the whirling dervish ceremony there until May 1967, when Israeli troops occupied the neighborhood.

> *If the appropriate time for loving comes,*
> *it will come exuberant like Damascus.*
> *And if the moment does not heed and fall for the heart,*
> *then it will be ruined like Aleppo.*

Rumi's legacy lives on in Syria, too. Wandering through the narrow alleys of the Old City of Damascus on my way to meet a revered Syrian Sufi master and poet, I stumbled upon an exhibit on Sufism in Syria with whirling dervish mannequins and old Mevlevi mystic documents in Arabic. Rumi's spiritual teacher, Shams of Tabriz, harbored a special love for the Umayyad Mosque in Syria: for him, Damascus was like paradise. Dervishes in Syria still perform the whirling ceremony in public in Rumi's honor.

> *Don't trouble yourself going to the garden.*
> *Look at what's inside the lover instead:*
> *Damascus and Ghouta, and the rose garden,*
> *and other beautiful places like Nayrab.*

While in Syria, I was invited to spend an all-night retreat alone in the tomb of the twelfth-century Spanish-born mystic philosopher Ibn Arabi, called the Shaykh of Shaykhs, whose godson, Qonavi, was Rumi's contemporary and colleague in Konya. Rumi embodied and transmitted the path of love in Konya, while Qonavi taught the path of religious knowledge. I thought of Rumi while meditating late at night alone in Ibn Arabi's underground tomb at the foot of Mount Qasiyun—a place that Rumi called "paradise on earth."

Damascus—what is it?
It is a paradise full of angels and heavenly virgins.
Rational people are astonished by those beautiful faces
*   and double chins.*

Rumi really is a global sensation: he pops up in the most unexpected places and times. While studying Sufism in Indonesia as a Fulbright Scholar, I opened up a magazine in a salon while getting a haircut and was surprised to find a big spread on Indonesian whirling dervishes in Java. I have even encountered Rumi while sailing through the skies. Traveling in the Islamic Republic of Iran as an invited speaker for Harvard, I was handed a newspaper by a flight attendant on a flight from Tabriz to Shiraz. As we took off for that famed city of mysticism, rose gardens, and poetry, I opened up the paper and found verses by Rumi:

TRAVELING ABROAD

Either this spiritual goal of mine will be reached
*   on this journey,*
or when I return home from the road.

*Maybe my devout desire depends
    on my travels abroad,
and only after I've journeyed,
I'll fulfill it at home.*

*With great effort and energy,
I will seek the beloved,
until I discover if I didn't need to seek at all.*

*How would his presence enter my ear,
unless I wander around the world?*

*How should I grasp the mystery of his company,
except after my long journeys?*

*God said that he is with us,
but he has sealed the heart,
so his presence may enter
indirectly not directly
the ear of the heart.*

*After you've journeyed far from home,
and performed the practices of the path,
the seal around your heart
will be removed.*

The next day, when our Harvard group entered the shrine complex of the Persian poet Saʻdi in Shiraz, we encountered three preteen refugee brothers from Afghanistan—who recited Rumi's poetry for us by heart. Children in both Afghanistan and Iran learn to memorize Rumi's verses from a very young age in school and the home.

Give the wars a rest,
and play the harps instead!
Then you may enrich the harps with melodies
from Isfahan and Iraq.

When I was journeying through Afghanistan on a one-woman mission of peace during the annual "killing season" of early spring, passing by American tanks on the highway under the discomfiting presence of aerostats and drones hovering above, I was surprised to spot a chiseled portrait of Rumi on the side of the main road leading to the brilliant shrine of Mazar-e Sharif—which just days before the Taliban had threatened to blow up. Wandering through a rural part of Balkh province, I was led through the winding, dusty roads of a small village to an old mud-brick dwelling that Afghans believe is connected to Rumi's family history.

In those ruins, a group of tiny Afghan kids no older than seven years old told me that I was in the house that belonged to "Rumi al-Balkhi." "Al-Balkhi!" they proclaimed, meaning "The One from Balkh," which today is the name of an Afghan province that in Rumi's time stretched into present-day Tajikistan. Under that crumbling mud-brick dome, a young Afghan girl named Parvane, whose name means "Butterfly" in Persian, recited for me a poem by Rumi that she had to memorize in school.

There is a treasure buried in the earth, concealed.
From the faithless and the faithful, concealed.
We saw that it was certainly love, concealed.
We became naked from what was concealed.

Like Rumi, she too was a child of wartime—singing of beauty in the midst of violence and celebrating the treasure

found in the ruins. Outside the maze of that quiet Afghan vil-
lage, the war still raged in all directions—but inside that home
full of sand, with Rumi's Persian verses wafting in the brisk
spring breeze, our hearts burned as one in remembrance of him.
Mystic love, you see, is always flickering in the hearts of the
lovers—even in endless war.

This is the gift of Rumi: a map for living virtuously and
loving fiercely in the midst of suffering so that we might un-
cover the treasure buried in our hearts and, together, experience
the transcendent potential of our illuminated and enlightened
souls.

O TRAVELER

O traveler, set not your heart upon a dwelling,
for you become weary at the time of attraction.

You have departed from many destinations,
from sperm to the season of youth.

Take it easy, so you may easily escape.
Give away generously, and find the true reward!

Hold fast to him, for he has taken firm hold of you.
He is the first and he is the last—now go find him!

His arrow causes quivers in the hearts of lovers,
as if he's skillfully drawing the bow of the rebab.

Be the lover Turk, Byzantine, or Arab,
in every language,
the call to righteousness is the same.

The wind is lamenting and singing to you:
"Come in my wake—follow me to the stream!
I was water. I became wind.
I have come to liberate
the thirsting ones
from this mirage."

Rumi wrote frequently about the merits of travel. He gives many examples from the Qur'an of the benefits and miracles that traveling in both the inner and outer realms can produce for an individual and humanity. Rumi also frequently references the Mi'raj, or "Night Journey," that the Prophet Muhammad took when he ascended through all seven levels of heaven on the back of the mythical winged creature Buraq toward the throne of God. The Prophet Muhammad's heavenly ascension began with the angels Gabriel and Michael, and the purification of his heart from error, doubt, and idolatry so that it could be filled with wisdom and belief instead. On his journey through the heavens to the throne of God, the Prophet Muhammad met many prophets, such as Adam, John the Baptist, Jesus, Joseph, Aaron, Moses, and Abraham. For Sufis, his ascension is the template for the purification of the heart and the soul's meditative and transcendent journey to mystic knowledge.

ALL THE TRAVELERS

Were the trees mobile,
they would not suffer the saw,
or be subject to unjust scars.

If the sun and moon stilled,
like a firm rock,
they would not bestow light upon us.

The Euphrates, the Tigris, and Amu Darya
would be so bitter,
if they were inert like the sea.

If air becomes trapped in a well,
it turns to poison.

As seawater travels up
through the air to the clouds,
it's purified from bitterness,
and becomes sweet like halva.

If fire desists from flaming and blazing,
it tapers off into death and annihilation
when turning to ash.

Look at Joseph of Canaan who traveled
from his father's house to Egypt
and became exceptional.

Look at Moses, son of Amram,
who went to Midian
from his mother's side
and became superior.

Look at Jesus of Mary,
who in his endless travels,
became, like spring water,
the manifestation of life and animation
and revived the dead.

Look at the Prophet Muhammad,
who left Mecca,

but campaigned with his army,
and returned as Mecca's lord.

Or look at the night of Mi'raj,
when the Prophet traveled on Buraq
through the heavens to such a height
he was only two bows' lengths from God—
or even less.

If you are not bored,
I could enumerate every single traveler
in the world in sets of two or three.

However, as I've already shown you a few,
you can conceive of the rest yourself.
Leave your habitual nature
and conditioning behind—
and travel toward the nature
and mood of God.

SUFISM: THE SCIENCE OF THE HEART

◆

Though there were pious ascetics and mystics in the earliest days of Islam, Islamic mysticism began to flourish in the ninth century in Basra, Baghdad, and along the Silk Road. In time, vibrant communities of Muslim mystics could be found in all corners of the Islamic world. During the "Golden Age of Sufism" (1150–1500), mystic practices and communities became more standardized and codified with the establishment and expansion of influential Sufi orders. In the nineteenth century, European Orientalists divorced Islamic mysticism from Islam in their scholarship, leading Western academics, writers, and readers to believe that what became known as Sufism—mystical practices focused on the inner spiritual dimensions, proper moral conduct, and esoteric knowledge of Islam—developed separately from Islam.

In your soul, there is a soul—seek that soul.
In the mountain of your body, there is a jewel—
seek that mine.

Sufism is understood today to be a mystic path of love followed by hearts of sincere devotion yearning to experience the divine essence directly through deep worship, meditation, and love. Sufism is the way of the pious—spiritual wayfarers dedicated to purifying their hearts and perfecting their characters. It is the road of vivacity, trod by awakened and thirsting hearts drunk on love of the divine—who Sufis refer to as "the beloved."

Don't let inner sorrow overtake you,
or the temptations of this world seize you.
Go, day and night, and pour the drink of love in your mouth—
before the final edict of truth closes your lips for good.

Sufism has been described by its practitioners for many centuries as a "science." Sufism is indeed a mystic science of both heart and soul. It is a science in how to live and how to love. Sufi mystics are said to be people of the heart with souls of purity. The esteemed medieval Persian philosopher Abu Hamid al-Ghazali (d. 1111) attempted to give his own definition of Sufism:

In general, how can men describe such a way as this? Its purity—the first of its requirements—is the total purification of the heart from everything other than God Most High. Its key, which is analogous to the beginning of the Prayer, is the utter absorption of the heart in the remembrance of God. Its end is being completely lost in God.

Dedicated to divine love, mystic lovers give up preoccupation with the self and the opinions of others to dive into the divine essence in each moment—and with each breath.

THE WAY

Someone asked: "What is the way?"
I said: "The way is to leave behind desire."

O, lover of the king! Know that your way
is to seek the pleasure of that great king!
When you seek the beloved's wish and will,
seeking your own desire is forbidden!

The whole spirit will transform into love of the beloved,
for this love is the cloister cell of the noble dervish!

His love is not less than the top of a mountain—
and for me, the mountaintop of his love is enough!

The cave where the friend is—is love!
The furnishing of the soul comes from his beauty.

Whatever purifies you is the correct path—
I will not define what it is.
Keep silent and be the shaykh of love.
For in the two worlds,
you are the imam.

In our daily suffering, born of our constant desires and never-ending dissatisfaction, we forget our hidden powers of love. As Rumi writes: "All of our suffering results from raw greed and from the desires of the self and its itching palate." The main goal of Sufism is to achieve loving union with the divine by detaching from the self and the desires of the ego. This is done by purifying the heart of negative characteristics through spiritual exercises—such as chanting the ninety-nine divine names of God, meditating, and ecstatic whirling. A mystic finds her cure from the sicknesses of fear, arrogance, greed, envy, hatred, desire, attachment, and self-centeredness by decorating her heart with beautiful qualities to draw spiritually nearer to the divine.

Worldly dominion is lawful to those who are self-indulgent,
but we are bound to the everlasting kingdom of love.

From a Sufi perspective, most people are sleepwalking through life with veils shielding their hearts from accepting the inevitable reality of death and the true nature of reality—thus they cannot awaken to the presence of the divine essence. As Rumi writes: "My religion is to live from love. Life lived from this soul and mind is shameful to me." Dervishes dare to try to throw off the thousands of veils separating them from perceiving the truth of divine reality before death strikes. Through the mystic alchemy of Sufism, a seeker's heart gradually transforms the pain of existence and the suffering of separation into sustained peace of mind and ecstatic union with the divine.

ALCHEMY LESSON

Learn spiritual alchemy from the messenger.
Whatever truth gives you, be satisfied.

The very moment you become happy in hardship,
the door of paradise will open wide.

If a messenger of sorrow comes to you,
embrace it like a friend.

A chill that comes from the beloved—
give it a warm and happy welcome.

Then sorrow will emerge from behind the veil,
sweet-voiced, tender, and charming.

Grab the edge of sorrow's veil,
for she is so beautiful,
but easy and a cheat.

In this lane, I'm the panderer—
I've pulled the veil from every beautiful face.

They all wear abhorrent veils,
so you'll think they're dragons.

I've had enough of my own soul—
so now I worship dragons.
If you're fed up with your soul,
then hear the dragons roar!

Now melancholy will never find me without laughter—
for without this medicine, I can't heal my pain.

Nothing is more blessed than sorrow,
for its reward has no end.

In cowardice,
you will find nothing.

I will be silent now,
so I don't utter a mistake.

For Rumi, the starting point of the spiritual path is pain—pain from self-preoccupation and from longing to be reunited with our source. Rumi's teacher, Shams of Tabriz, said about the aching heart of a spiritual seeker: "Hasn't it been said, 'I am near to those whose hearts have been broken'?" Sufis seek to liberate themselves from the disappointments of desire, the disease of ambition, and the worship of wealth. A dervish searches day and night for a cure for a life lived in fear, ignorance, and the illusion of separation. Pain, as Rumi explains, is the portal through which a dervish becomes a perfected human being.

> Pain must be a dervish's actual belonging.
> And then, in the midst of pain, he must become a man.
> In every direction, they build yet again another monastery.
> The universe is a monastery—there only need be
>   a true human being.

For a Sufi, peace and fulfillment are found in the process of becoming a real human being, instead of trying to endlessly satisfy the never-ending desires of the ego. Rumi asks: Where are the real human beings? In all directions on earth, we can see the minarets of mosques and the towers of monasteries—but a good human being is much harder to find, and a perfected one even rarer still.

> They ask me: "Why are you in pain all over?
> Why do you shout and sing? Why is your face pale?"
> I say: "Don't tell me what I do is a mistake.
> Go, look at the moon of her face, and you'll see the problem."

Becoming a true human being is achieved through becoming a servant to the divine and all humanity. As Rumi explains, a Sufi avoids causing any trouble to anyone or indulging in the passions and whims of the ego. Instead, the mystic seeks to benefit other people and feel oneness with all creation to draw nearer to the Creator of all.

On the path of oneness, what is the difference
between worship and sin?
In the tavern lane, what is the difference
between dervish and king?
What does it matter if the face of a wandering dervish
is light or dark?
On the turret of the highest heaven, what is the difference
between sun and moon?

Seeking the sweetness of oneness, a Sufi frees herself from judgment, duality, and distinctions. She instead fixes her gaze on the truth of unseen mystic realms—the invisible world of the spirit beyond the physical world and our sensory perceptions of it. The happiness of the Sufi flows from within—not from the material external world.

Be happy—for a Sufi is good-natured.
A Sufi is happy from within himself.
A Sufi is pure—sorrow does not settle upon him.
A Sufi must be like Kay-Khosraw and Kay-Qobad.

Here, Rumi references two Persian kings mentioned in the eleventh-century Persian epic the *Shahnameh* (*The Persian Book of Kings*) by the poet Ferdowsi. Rumi drew inspiration in content and style from this legendary epic, which tells the history of the Persians through mythology. In fact, from the twelfth century onward, Seljuk rulers of Rum adopted the names of legendary Persian kings, like Kay-Khosraw and Kay-Qobad, and even decorated the walls of Konya's citadel with verses from this acclaimed poetic masterpiece.

We are the ones happy with the wine without the grail—
every morning filled with light and every evening full of joy.
There is no conclusion for us, they say.
We are the ones happy without conclusion.

Rumi speaks often in his poetry about being intoxicated with love—love of the divine. Drunk on this love, a Sufi heart is always brimming with light and joy—and there is no end to it.

THE BELOVED IS COMING

O sorrow,
go out from my heart—
for the benevolence of my friend is coming.

O heart,
you can get lost too—
for my beloved is coming.

I do not call the friend "happiness,"
since he has gone beyond happiness.

Shame is coming to me from happiness,
because of the lavishness of his love.

O Muslims, begin anew being Muslim,
for even unbelief becomes like a believer,
when shamed by my beloved's beauty.

O gratitude,
go away—

for my blessings go beyond
the bounds of gratitude.

I don't even wish for patience,
though sometimes it makes for
a good coworker.

O all forms—
go away,
since new forms have come!

All your flags will be turned upside down,
for that lavish one is coming!

He's tearing apart the door and walls of the heart,
because his immensity can't be contained
or fit through the doorframe—
so he's coming in through the walls.

There is no clear consensus among scholars about where the term "Sufism" originated. Some believe it comes from the Persian word for "pure" (*saf*), while others maintain it derives from the Arabic word for "wool" (*suf*), since early Muslim mystics wore wool as an ascetic practice of tribulation, mark of identification, and act of imitation (in emulation of the Prophet Muhammad who reportedly wore a woolen garment). The wearing of uncomfortable, hot, and itchy wool was seen by some early Muslim mystics as a spiritual trial that would train a dervish to suppress his ego and desire for comfort. Later in Rumi's life, when plunged into profound grief after the mysterious disappearance of his spiritual teacher, Rumi traded his silk judge's robe for a dark blue linen cloak, which he wore until his death.

He is a Sufi, and he has flung off
his cloak in ecstasy!
How should he return again
to that discarded mantle?

The woolen clothes of early mystics projected a life defined by humility, modesty, and sincerity. Because woolen clothes signaled virtue, some dervish manuals cautioned Sufis not to become arrogant after donning the cloak. As a result, these manuals suggested that not all who sought to wear a Sufi cloak should be allowed to wear it. The manuals even provided qualifications, provisions, and regulations related to wearing it to prevent the cloak from being worn as a means of pretension by spiritual impostors. In the following verses, Rumi warns against blind imitation and the greedy pretension of some spiritual practitioners—insincere dervishes and fraudulent masters.

SPIRITUAL IMPOSTORS

Oh, many impostors pretend to practice a spiritual way of life,
while they haven't seen anything other than the Sufi's wool
in the way of true men of spirit.

Many arrogant hypocrites with limited practice
have learned nothing from spiritual masters
other than empty talk and bragging.

Each one with a staff in his hand says:
"I am Moses,"
or breathes on fools, saying:
"I am Jesus."

Watch out! There will be a day when the touchstone of honesty
tests you to see if you're qualified
with the sincerity of the honest ones!

You can ask the rest of the story from your master—
such greedy impostors are blind and mute.

You were eager to search for all kinds of knowledge,
but instead you lost everything.
This makes you like idiot cattle—
perfect prey for wolves.

You heard only the shape and surface of truth,
and translated what you learned by rote
into your own ignorant words, like parrots.

Rumi cautions that a dervish must not just parrot a fraudulent impostor or blindly follow spiritual masters like cattle—otherwise, they will fall prey to "wolves" like greed, jealousy, and pride, which can attack and devour the splendor and sincerity of a spiritual seeker's pure heart and spiritual aspirations.

Let the lover be drunk all year and infamous!
Let him be crazy, frenzied, and lovesick!
With sobriety, we suffer sorrow about everything,
but when we become drunk—what will be, will be!

One word that cycles through Rumi's poetry perhaps more than any other is a Persian word for "sorrow." It can also be translated as grief, longing, pain, affliction, anguish, heartache, and yearning, depending on the context. Nestled in the lap of love, the lover knows not sorrow connected to the material world—a Sufi, after all, is just passing through the house of life. Rumi often portrays the mystic as transcending earthly sorrow, but he also writes about how sorrow serves a purpose, as it makes room for us to experience new delights. In his words, "Whatever sorrow sheds or takes from the heart, it will truly bring better in exchange."

In the tradition of classical Persian poetry, sorrow is epitomized by the figure of a lover crying out in painful separation from his beloved—a desperate and vulnerable state that purifies and intensifies his love. Similarly, a dervish is plunged into sweet sorrow when feeling distant from the divine—but when reunited, all sorrows disappear! The bittersweet sorrow in Rumi's poetry is intended to inspire a dervish's heart to long for greater spiritual intimacy with her mystic master and deepen her longing for reunion with the divine.

Vulnerability enables a dervish to get closer to her beloved, but the assertion and practice of vulnerability with one's spiritual master and in one's relationship with the divine is no easy feat. Outwardly, a dervish must be vulnerable and honest with her shaykh and fellow dervishes in sharing her anxieties, fears, and egotistic desires. Inwardly, she must be in touch with her yearning for closeness and dependence on the beloved. As Rumi says, "Increase your need quickly, O needy one, so the sea of generosity may swell in bounty." It is our brokenness that ushers in mercy and blessings and compels us to draw nearer to one another and the divine beloved.

In my heart, sit down sometime like a secret and don't go.
In my mind, sit down sometime like a turban and don't go.
Even if the crowd has all gone, O my idol, don't go.
O my companion and drinking partner, don't go.

Divine mercy surges when neediness is felt and expressed. According to a saying of the Prophet Muhammad, if we take a step toward God, he will rush to meet us: "Whoever comes to me walking, I will come to him running." Every moment, every breath, is an opportunity to become free from the shackles of our self and encounter the divine.

Every particle of the world, one by one,
is for fools bondage,
and for spiritual masters—liberation.

By nurturing one's love for the divine through study, prayer, and meditation, a Sufi undoubtedly experiences greater intimacy with the beloved and deeper gratitude for the abundance of blessings that follow. A mystic endeavors to devote each inhale and each exhale to love and remembrance of the beloved. Self and world must be sacrificed in the quest for ecstatic union with the divine.

THE NEWS

It was night,
but only for strangers.

My night is day,
because of the fair face of the friend.

If the whole world were overtaken by thorns,
we'd drown in a rose garden of the beloved.

And if the whole world fell to ruins and was rebuilt,
my heart would still be drunk and ruined, my love.

Since the news is all depressing,
the absence of news becomes
the source of real news!

Rumi adhered to the obligatory outward practices of Islam, but he also engaged in mystic modes of spirituality, such as whirling in ecstasy, playing sacred music, meditating on the ninety-nine names of God, contemplating the divine, and writing devotional poetry. These spiritual exercises kept his awareness and consciousness immersed in deep meditative states in the inner mosque of the heart. Dervishes, you see, are always on a journey—traveling through the hidden chambers of the heart to explore different spiritual states and reach new mystic heights.

Hide my secrets within your soul.
Hide my spiritual states from yourself too.

Rumi writes frequently about traveling through different spiritual states and stations. A spiritual state is a mystical moment or spiritual experience that brings a dervish a momentary taste of ecstatic connection with the divine. As al-Ghazali, the great twelfth-century Persian philosopher, theologian, jurist, and mystic, noted in his account of his spiritual crisis that prompted him to leave his prestigious teaching position in Baghdad to wander instead as a dervish in Damascus and Jerusalem in search of mystic knowledge: "I knew with certainty that the Sufis were masters of states, not purveyors of words, and that I had learned all I could by way of theory." For Muslim mystics, a spiritual state is transient: it is a change in being, seeing, or feeling—such as blissful bewilderment or overpowering ecstasy—that expands the heart of the dervish but is not sustained. It is a gift of grace—catalyzed by the divine.

A spiritual station, on the other hand, is referred to as a "station" for the dervish usually "arrives" at it through practice and personal effort. A spiritual station is a stop on the heart's journey back to the source on the caravan of love; the "station" can be returned to and built upon. The spiritual station endures, whereas a spiritual state is fleeting. A station may manifest as an achievement of humility, detachment, or fear of God's power. As Rumi explains:

The state is like the display of the beautiful bride,
and the station is like retreating in private with the bride.

Sufis seek to taste different spiritual experiences and achieve transcendent spiritual states in their attempt to unveil the truth of divine reality. They know that intellectual discourse can only go so far, as true divine love must be felt with the heart, not grasped through the mind or intellect.

There are many people of states among the Sufis,
yet it is rare to find people of stations in their midst.

Though Rumi was a master of language, he knew that words, like the intellect, were veils to perceiving the truth. Rumi, like other Sufis at the time, was often criticized and slandered for religious innovation and heresy. For this reason, some Sufis, including Rumi, insisted on the need for mystics to conceal their inner spiritual states and avoid sharing those states in detail or displaying them in public in whirling ceremonies and meditation circles.

Secrets—I cannot give away.
Even under threat, I cannot share them.

Something inside of me gives me joy.
I cannot put my finger on it.

Medieval Sufi ethics distinguished dervishes from other Muslims in several respects: the emphasis on a renunciatory mode of piety, the imperative to veil one's piety from others, the merits of Sufi companionship over association with others, and the Sufi tradition of wearing wool. Seeking to be in constant communion with the divine with every breath and each step, a mystic yearns with every atom of their being to please God in striving to become a perfected human being with a heart of purity, compassion, and, above all—love.

RETREAT

◆

The mystic gems embedded in Rumi's poetry are not merely the fossilized remains of a medieval way of life; their lasting brilliance is reflected in the living tradition of Islamic mysticism as practiced by people all over the world. Today, mystic hearts from all walks of life around the world follow in Rumi's footsteps. Doctors, professors, lawyers, dry cleaners, artists, students, the poor—all are welcome in Rumi's caravan of love, which has been attracting hearts for centuries, from his lifetime to the present day.

There are countless Sufi orders in the world today that follow different lineages of spiritual visionaries back to the Prophet Muhammad. In addition to the Mevlevi Sufi Order dedicated to sharing Rumi's gift and honoring his memory, there are the Qadiriyya, Shadhuliyya, Tijaniyya, Naqshbandiyya, Rifaʿiyya, Chishtiyya, Khalwatiyya, Jerrahiyya, and Khatmiyya Sufi Orders, along with many other Sufi orders around the globe that follow their own mystic lineages of spiritual transmission.

This solitude is worth more than a thousand lives.
This freedom is worth more than the kingdom of the world.
Being in retreat with truth for just one moment
is worth more than life and the world—than this or that.

Though Rumi was married and an active and revered religious public figure in his day, he also treasured solitude. Rumi writes often of the benefits of spiritual seclusion and retreat in his poems. During his time, mystics would do meditation retreats for 40 days or even 1,001 days in a small meditation cell. Dervishes would separate from their families and friends to spend their days praying, contemplating the divine, reciting the ninety-nine divine names of God (such as "The Patient One," "The Loving One," etc.) with prayer beads, reading the Qur'an, playing musical instruments, composing mystical poetry, and whirling in spiritual ecstasy. During a spiritual retreat, a mystic would eat and sleep very little; such a retreat was seen as an ascetic act of solitude and a noble cultivation of intimacy with the beloved.

SECLUSION

That vizier gave a shout from within:
O disciples, may this from me be known.

That Jesus gave this message to me:
Be separated from all your family and friends.

Sit alone and meditate before a wall—
choose seclusion from even your own existence.

While on retreat, a dervish would meditate on the principles of the Sufi path, such as complete trust in God, total acceptance of one's situation, the cultivation of nonattachment, the oneness of being, and the centrality of sincerity. Such a difficult inner pilgrimage through the desert of solitude and into the abode of the heart is guided by a mystic master. As part of his retreat, a Sufi shares his revelatory dreams and waking visions (in which prophets, angelic beings, deceased Sufi shaykhs, or living mystic masters may appear) with his spiritual teacher, who interprets the dreams spiritually and gives the dervish guidance based on what the dreams reveal about the inner state of the dervish's heart. Spiritual masters interpret all these otherworldly visitations through the prism of the heart.

Spiritual encounters in the invisible realm are thought to be signs of a Sufi growing in nearness to prophetic consciousness and the divine. In the words of the Prophet Muhammad, regarding those who have seen him in dreams: "He who has seen me has truly seen me." After all, to a Sufi, the invisible world is real, and the visible world is an illusion.

> *Your spirit must become very tired.*
> *You must become conspicuous by this and that.*
> *If you're human then get along with humankind,*
> *and if you're an angel—toward the sky you must fly!*

Even though Rumi sings the praises of retreat and solitude, he also urges us to get along with humankind, as we are all a part of humankind. After all, in his words, "All the people in the world are prisoners, in expectation of death in a world that is passing away." Rumi encourages us to exercise patience and practice compassion in the face of humanity's many limitations, shortcomings, and injustices. We cannot escape from what we are or turn our backs on humanity in disgust, contempt, or hopelessness. Those who are more angelic, however, may aim their hearts solely toward the divine, leaving the world completely behind.

Today, at Rumi's shrine complex in Konya, visitors can see a meditation cell decorated with Ottoman calligraphy in the buildings adjacent to his tomb and imagine what it would have been like to engage in such a lengthy spiritual retreat in the thirteenth century. The dervish begging bowls on display serve as a reminder of the humility and charity of medieval mystics. The life-size dioramas of whirling dervishes and dervishes cooking in the kitchen bring to life Rumi's poems on cooking—which depict dervishes as chickpeas being purified through boiling and simmering in the fire and flavors of love.

In Rumi's poetry, he implores one to seek seclusion from one's own life and to retreat from the self—to separate from one's own ambition and identity and just *be*. While we tend to think of movement as freedom, Rumi suggests that it is in solitude and stillness where the true liberation of the mind and heart can be found.

> *For a while, we meditated among the humans.*
> *From them, no color nor scent of loyalty did we detect.*
> *It's best that we hide from the view of the crowd,*
> *like water in steel and fire in stone.*

Though a Sufi has compassion and patience for humankind, he also hides from the crowd—choosing solitude and the company of mystic companions instead. Sufis try to be "in" the world but not "of" the world—participating in the daily affairs of life without being attached to praise, success, or reputation. This is why Rumi's teacher, Shams of Tabriz, called himself a "stranger" to this world: he was just passing through, unattached to the world and the self.

> *I am happy, because I'm free from worldly happiness.*
> *I am drunk, because even if I don't drink wine, I'm happy.*
> *I have no need to know about the state of another.*
> *Congratulations to me for this hidden brilliance.*

The happiness of the mystic comes from within. As the Qur'an states, "The enjoyment of this world is nothing but the enjoyment of delusions." Worldly happiness holds no interest for the spiritually inclined. A dervish's inner state is not influenced, shaped, or touched by the circumstances of the outside world. A Sufi is not preoccupied with the shortcomings, opinions, judgments, or failings of others.

> *O you, whose soul is distracted with the shortcomings of others,*
> *and has uttered excuses for their souls—*
> *even if a flood of suffering invaded the world,*
> *it would be nothing to me—*
> *because I would be drunk and passed out.*

Rumi is not literally drunk and passed out—he is drunk on love! Not even the worst disaster can touch or spoil an ecstatic state of love. Being drunk on love is one thing—but being passed out from it is a whole other level! The intoxication of love can lead to a blackout of selfhood! Become drunk and passed out on love, Rumi suggests, instead of poisoned by the problems of the self, others, and the world. The extinguishing of the self in deep love is like a momentary death—until we sober up and rejoin the world.

O BROTHER

> *O brother—a lover must have pain!*
> *Where is your pain?*

> *Patience and honesty require a real man.*
> *Where is such a man?*

> *For how long will your meditation*
> *be dispirited?*
> *For how long will your contemplation*

be stuck on worldly affairs?
Where are your passionate cries
and sallow face?

I do not seek alchemy for gold—
where is just one deserving disciple?
Why can I only find a warm and healthy face?

I am not well or warm.
Where there are chills and pain—
give me that.

Rumi's verses force us to reflect: How do we choose to spend our precious, limited time on this earth? Fixated on ourselves? Worried about what others think of us? Disappointed with the shortcomings of others? Determined to overlook or change their faults? Rumi shows us that when we focus on the perceived failures of others, we rob ourselves of the opportunity to lose ourselves in love and connect to the presence of the divine.

Rumi continually implores us to awaken—to live consciously so that each moment can be an experience and offering of love. He exclaims, "Today is the Resurrection! O my soul, don't sit down!" For a dervish, every day is Judgment Day, and every moment is the Resurrection—an opportunity to die to the self and be reborn. Living consciously and lovingly, for Rumi, is a process of retreating from the world by leaving behind our ego, worldly attachments, and temptations. Even the promise of heavenly reward must be abandoned in favor of the here and now. As Rumi writes, "You are a Sufi, so don't say the name of the past."

Turning their backs on darkness, Sufis focus solely on the light—the illumination of love. The vanity and violence of the world are not their concern. As Rumi writes, "We escape from bondage—we are not in bondage to the world." To be truly free, we must break the chains of ordinary existence, conditioning, opinion, and habit. We must liberate ourselves from reputation and reward. Free from all attachments and the shackles of the world, a soul finally realizes there is, in reality, nothing to leave behind. All is empty; the only reality is love!

MY SULTAN

My sultan! My sultan!
And in my heart and soul,
my faith!

If you breathe into me,
I become alive.
What is just one soul?
You are my soul times a hundred!

Bread without you is poison to me—
not bread.

You are my water,
as well as my bread.

Poison from you becomes
an antidote for me—
my candy and gifted sugar.

You are my garden, meadow, and paradise—
my cypress and laughing jasmine!

You are also my king, as well as my moon—
my ruby, as well as my mine.

I became silent,
so you could explain it to me—
for you are my reasoning
when it comes to speech.

* * *

Will your pain accept a cure? Never!
Or desire ever desert you? Never!
You say: The seed of patience is cultivated in the heart.
I say: It may grow, but it will never sprout.

"This is the shrine of Sultan Mehmet II, who conquered Constantinople in 1453 at the young age of twenty-one," Ibrahim said, pointing at a white turban atop a giant sarcophagus and whispering a prayer. I had met Ibrahim—a wise and mysterious Sufi whose intense and knowing eyes, white hair, and matching beard brought Donald Sutherland to mind—the night before at an authentic whirling ceremony in Istanbul.

"But this is not why I brought you here. Come, follow me," he said, leading me out of the mosque gates onto a bustling, unpaved road. As we walked past a butcher shop and vegetable stand to arrive at an unmarked door, Ibrahim greeted everyone by name and with a quick but intentional tip of his hand as a wave.

After trudging up several flights, we arrived at an arched door, in front of which were twenty pairs of shoes, all perfectly arranged and facing the same direction. For Sufis, even shoes must be placed with sincere and loving intention, since being a dervish is all about proper etiquette and ethical conduct. On the dervish path, intention and good manners are seen as the foundation of all other actions and spiritual aspirations.

Opening the door, Ibrahim revealed an apartment that reminded me more of a hippie hangout than the other homes I had visited in Istanbul—with its low, wooden-paneled ceilings, embroidered floor cushions, and heavy cloud of cigarette smoke. Every inch was decorated with the finest Sufi decor: frame drums ornamented with Arabic calligraphy, photographs of revered Sufi masters, and delicate reed flutes of mystic musicians.

"This is Baba," Ibrahim said, gesturing to the shaykh, whose wavy, silver hair and chiseled, tan face gave him the look of a leading man. As I walked over to meet the shaykh, whose turbans from three different Sufi orders were displayed in a niche above the cushions where he held court, he looked familiar to me—yet I had no memories of ever meeting him.

"Baba teaches *sema*, the sacred ceremony of the whirling dervishes," Ibrahim said. Though I knelt and tried to kiss Baba's hand, as I had seen other dervishes do as a sign of respect, Baba snatched his hand away from me in a gesture of humility and smiled.

In Sufism, the relationship between a master and disciple is intense and intimate. A student is expected to imitate the *adab* (proper conduct, manners, and ethical behavior) of her teacher. A dervish disciple is an apprentice to her master. This apprenticeship is spiritual and practical in nature. Spiritually, the dervish spends countless hours at the side of her master, benefiting from the teacher's wisdom, learning from the master's knowledge, and imitating the shaykh's manner of devotional practice and relating to others. Practically, the dervish serves the master in various roles and, in doing so, learns the benefits of selfless service and loving generosity.

After our greetings and introductions, Baba gestured to the low, round table in the middle of the room and invited me to eat with him and his dervish disciples.

Before us was a large bowl filled with hearty pieces of beef and a medley of vegetables poured over rice. The only other female was an elderly, seemingly psychotic Turkish woman whose high-pitched staccato voice was unlike any I had ever heard. Though I could tell she was mocking me in Turkish, I had no idea what she was saying about me—but I found her charming and entertaining nonetheless.

"A lot of people have encountered the priceless qualities of the Sufi path through books—however, there is a difference between discussing these texts philosophically and living Sufism practically," Baba said. He explained that the mystic path requires time and a sincere intention. It cannot be learned or understood in a day: it is an experiential path. The learning is in the *being*.

"Sufism, you see, is not just a word, but a science of living; it is just like psychotherapy, but it goes a step beyond therapy, because it opens up the heart and helps us to get in touch with our deepest self, so that we can be true friends with the beloved," Baba explained to me. It all sounded very nice, but I wasn't sure I had what it took.

Sufis know and accept that every human being, especially those drawn to the spiritual path, is broken and in need of healing. The Sufi path attracts souls yearning for a sense of wholeness and connection to repair the brokenness or incompleteness at the core of their being. Through the mystic path, a soul can return to its original state of goodness and natural ability to sense the presence of the divine. After all, the ultimate goal of the Sufi path is to return back to the beginning—to the state of grace at birth. But, as Rumi experienced in his own life, the transformative journey back to the divine and one's own natural state of grace must be guided by a spiritual master.

"Listen, we take human beings when they are raw. The Sufi path is here to teach you qualities that are hard to find, like patience, hard work, love, compassion for others, and tolerance, since its main goal is to produce perfected human beings who understand that service to humanity is the greatest form of worship," Baba said.

A Sufi master, he explained, guides a mystic disciple through the process of purifying the heart to relinquish the ego and its desires and seek union with the divine. Through the loving heart of a shaykh, a spiritual seeker is initiated into a mystic chain of transmission from heart to heart that reaches back to the Prophet Muhammad. As an exemplar in moral and ethical conduct, a Sufi master models for a dervish proper etiquette in imitation of the Prophet Muhammad. Sufism takes its moral and ethical principles from the Qur'an and the sayings, conduct, and character of the Prophet Muhammad, whom Sufis see as the paragon of virtue.

After I shared with Baba one of my mind-blowing mystic dreams related to Rumi, Baba offered me a unique invitation—much to my surprise.

"I would like to invite you to live here for forty days in a traditional Sufi retreat," Baba said.

While forty-day retreats were standard fare in the classical period of Sufism, I knew the practice had been abandoned for centuries. Extended retreats are no longer practiced as they once were in Rumi's day. Although I was intrigued by the novelty of his suggestion, I declined, since I didn't have enough money to stay in Turkey for more than a few days.

"Don't worry about that; you can have the apartment below—it's yours; I give it to you," Baba said.

Sipping sweet Turkish tea from a miniature glass, I deliberated about whether or not to accept his generous offer. Was I committed enough to do an intensive retreat with a Sufi shaykh? Or could I just be content to pontificate about Sufism—without really embodying and practicing it?

"The foundation of any spiritual journey or retreat is self-discipline," Baba said.

A frightening abundance of self-discipline had helped me master a dozen languages and willfully starve myself into a medical crisis in college. But the willful self-discipline I had first mastered at a young age while training in ballet with legends like Gelsey Kirkland and competing at the national level in sports was focused on perfecting my "self," instead of relinquishing my self. Could a forty-day retreat help me liberate myself—from myself?

A will to live had seemed to elude me from my very first days, when I was hospitalized as a baby for failing to thrive. My body and soul were still in desperate need of healing, care, and love.

"The only thing that is necessary to receive the blessings of Sufism is an interest and willingness to learn. However, from what we can see, people in Western Europe, America, and Australia live in a culture and society that is very fast, and many learn simply and quickly and strive for short-term solutions. This way of being is not in accordance with Sufism," Baba explained.

A retreat, he explained, would help me cultivate patience. Patience is a theme that courses through Rumi's poetry. In fact, patience and gratitude have been central themes in Islamic mysticism throughout the centuries. Patience is even considered half of the religion of Islam. Rumi says, "Be patient, for patience is the key to joyous relief." The Qur'an also notes the importance of patience when facing challenges—after each trial, it reminds us, comes ease.

I felt there may be some deeply buried seed of patience in my heart, but getting it to sprout would take more than forty days—more like a lifetime. As Baba explained, mysticism is not a momentary solution or feel-good-fix; it is a lifelong practice and commitment.

A sentence of forty days was nothing compared to the retreats at the time of Rumi, when the standard initiation retreat—which consisted of whirling, praying, meditating, charity, music, and poetry—lasted 1,001 days. A month devoted to *being* rather than *doing* sounded enticing but challenging.

To Rumi, the foundation of knowledge is commitment. I wondered if I could survive the full forty days in an apartment with a dervish community of mostly men.

"Whoever wants to go deep in Sufism needs to allocate enough time to do that—such a person, in addition to having a deep desire to learn, also needs to act with heartfelt intentions and a hunger to understand reality," Baba told me.

Could I exorcise the self-critical chatter in my mind and behave with compassion instead of contempt toward my suffering soul? Could I build up my low self-esteem and will to live with discipleship, spiritual community, and whirling meditation? Would a dervish retreat help me glue together the fragmented shards of my self and become present and whole?

"Well," Baba said, "what do you think?"

"I'll do it," I said, with the knowledge that I could always leave voluntarily if the retreat proved too trying.

"Wonderful," Baba replied, as Hafiz, an attentive and gentle dervish in his twenties with dirty-blond hair, sallow skin, and subtle mutton chops—who had impressively memorized the entire Qur'an—grabbed my bags to take me to my new apartment downstairs.

COME TO THE RUINS

You are still at the mental stage
of arranging your shoes and turban.
So how can you even think of holding
the precious cup in your hand?

By my soul, come for a moment to the ruins.
You are a human being, a person, and you have a soul.

Come and pawn your Sufi cloak
to the wine-seller of primordial time—
for before water and clay,
the primordial past was in a drunken state.

Beggar, gnostic, and dervish—yet still sober?
These names are mere metaphors—
you're just imagining things!

Are not whirling and drinking wine
* from the wine-giver*
the work of the dervish?

Are not profit and loss—
more and less—
the work of the merchant?

Come, tell us, what is the primordial covenant?
Eternal pleasure.

Don't agonize yourself pretending to limp
when you're ambling swiftly on the way.

Why do you bind a head
that has no pain?
And why do you pretend
your healthy body
is sick?

THE ROOT OF SPIRITUAL PRACTICE

A human being is like a tree whose root is commitment—
you should rigorously tend to this root.

A failed commitment is like a rotted root,
unable to produce any grace or fruit.

Though the branches and leaves
of the date palm are green,
if its root is corrupted,
its greenness won't save it.

However, if it has no green leaves,
but the root is healthy,
it will grow hundreds of leaves.

Don't let a person's knowledge deceive you,
and notice if they're committed—
for knowledge is like the shell,
and commitment the kernel.

* * *

O melancholic one, go and pursue melancholy—
be frenzied in the hue of your melancholic heart.
With your own shadow you're at war,

because of your bad character.
Your own shadow is your enemy—so go be alone!

It wasn't until Hafiz pushed open the door of my new apartment that I realized I would have an entire floor of the building to myself. This was no solitary cell. Hafiz set down my bags as I walked to the stained-glass windows and peered down at the dusty street below.

I spotted the bakery, where a baker was selling a piece of baklava to an excited child, and a butcher was carving up the carcass of a cow. I felt like I was about to be carved up, too—my desires dissected and the secrets of my heart revealed.

Out of the corner of my eye, I saw Hafiz down the long hallway waving me over to inspect the bathroom. "Come here," he said in French, which was the language we used to communicate.

"Is it all right?" he said, pointing to the Turkish-style toilet—otherwise known as a hole in the ground.

"It's great," I said, knowing my upcoming spiritual journey would cause far more discomfort than a squat toilet ever would.

"I'll leave you alone to freshen up," Hafiz said. Gazing at my reflection in the mirror, while scrubbing off the film of fatigue from a long day of surprises, I tried to discern if I was in my right mind. How was I going to explain a forty-day retreat to my family and friends? Would they think I was being held hostage? Or perhaps joining a cult? Was it insane to live among only Turkish men—most of whom were strangers—for forty days?

Being in the "now," as the Sufi path demanded, felt impossible. I felt like an impostor. My thoughts were always hung on despair and fixated on criticizing myself. On top of that, I was very depressed about the state of the world and humanity in general. I wondered: Would a forty-day retreat help to heal me from my melancholy?

When I went back upstairs to thank Baba for the apartment, he and his dervishes were on his balcony, huddled around a white plastic table—smoking and drinking Turkish coffee. As the call to prayer emanated from the Ottoman minarets of Fatih Mosque, towering directly above us, hundreds of seagulls were circling the mosque's cupola.

"See, even the birds whirl," Baba said, pointing to the seagulls. Everywhere Baba turned his gaze, he saw whirling dervishes in disguise.

"Can you hear what they're saying?" Baba said. While I'm a polyglot by nature, their cooing was unintelligible to my untrained ear.

"They're saying, 'Allah, Allah, Allah'—listen, and you'll hear all creatures crying out to their Creator," Baba said. In the Qur'an, even the birds and mountains join the Prophet David in song.

ONE SOUL

The moment is like a cool breeze when we're sitting
  on the veranda,
you and I—with two forms and two faces,
but one soul, you and I.

The gifts of the garden and the breath of the birds
will give us the water of life,
the moment when we come into the garden,
you and I.

The stars of the sky will come as our spectators,
and to them we'll reveal the moon itself,
you and I.

You and I, without "you" and "I,"
from the heights of joy will become united—
blissful and free from idle talk
and distracting nonsense, you and I.

All the parrots of the sky will be consuming sugar
in the place where we'll laugh in such a way,
you and I.

This is even more amazing: that you and I
    are in one corner here,
yet in this moment we are both in Iraq and Khorasan,
you and I.

We have one form on this earth,
and another in eternal paradise
and the land of sugar,
you and I.

Though Rumi enjoyed the spiritual benefits of occasional re-
treat and seclusion, he was against the concept of monasticism.
One should not shut oneself off from the world, he felt, because
without the vices, tests, and troubles of the world, one has no
opportunity to develop spiritually and practice refining one's
conduct, character, and compassion. It is in the battle against
the ego that a spiritual wayfarer can refine her spiritual state
and polish her heart.

TURN YOUR HEART AWAY

Turn your heart away from tearing out your feathers
just to abstain from seeming vain—
because a battle is conditioned to the presence of a foe.

If there is no foe, a battle is impossible,
and if there is no lust in you,
there'll be no obedience either.

There's no need for self-restraint,
when you don't desire.
And without an enemy,
there's no need for your resolve.

Now look—don't go castrate yourself,
and become a monk,
for chastity is obtained through lust.

It's impossible to resist sensuality
without having an urge,
just as you can't heroically
wage war against the dead.

It's said in the Qur'an to spend—so get trading!
Without sufficient income, there can be no giving.

Though the imperative "Spend!" is said absolutely,
you should read it as: "Earn some, and then spend!"

Likewise, when the king commands you to be patient,
there must first be some restless desire in you
from which you should turn away.

Thus, God invites us to eat
to trigger our appetite—
after which, we're called
not to overindulge or waste.

THE NINETY-NINE NAMES
OF GOD

◆

In their daily life and when on retreat, dervishes meditate on the ninety-nine names of God in Arabic with the help of prayer beads. They try to integrate the essence of each name into their own being to cleanse their minds of negative thoughts, inspire their souls, and deepen their heart's meditative states. Depending on the guidance of their particular mystic master, dervishes may recite one attribute at a time, such as compassion, gratitude, patience, or love, or a combination of several names at once. In all directions and with each breath, a mystic tries to perceive, feel, and embody the attributes of the beautiful names of God.

Ar-Rahman	The Compassionate
Ar-Rahim	The Merciful
Al-Malik	The King
Al-Quddus	The Holy
As-Salam	The Source of Peace
Al-Mu'min	The Inspirer of Faith
Al-Muhaymin	The Guardian
Al-'Aziz	The Victorious One
Al-Jabbar	The Compeller
Al-Mutakabbir	The Sublime
Al-Khaliq	The Creator

Al-Bari'	The Maker
Al-Musawwir	The Fashioner
Al-Ghaffar	The Most Forgiving
Al-Qahhar	The Subduer
Al-Wahhab	The Giver
Ar-Razzaq	The Provider
Al-Fattah	The Opener
Al-'Alim	The Knower of All
Al-Qabid	The Constrictor
Al-Basit	The Expander
Al-Khafid	The Reducer
Ar-Rafi'	The Exalter
Al-Mu'izz	The Bestower of Honors
Al-Mudhill	The Dishonorer
As-Sami	The All-Hearing
Al-Basir	The All-Seeing
Al-Hakam	The Judge
Al-'Adl	The Just
Al-Latif	The Gentle
Al-Khabir	The All-Aware
Al-Halim	The Forbearing
Al-'Azim	The Magnificent
Al-Ghafur	The Always Forgiving
Ash-Shakur	The Rewarder of Gratitude
Al-'Ali	The Highest
Al-Kabir	The Greatest
Al-Hafiz	The Preserver
Al-Muqit	The Nourisher
Al-Hasib	The Accounter
Al-Jalil	The Majestic
Al-Karim	The Generous
Ar-Raqib	The Watchful

Al-Mujib	The Responder
Al-Wasi'	The Boundless
Al-Hakim	The Wise One
Al-Wadud	The Loving One
Al-Majid	The Glorious One
Al-Ba'ith	The Resurrector
Ash-Shahid	The Witness
Al-Haqq	The Truth
Al-Wakil	The Trustee
Al-Qawi	The Strong
Al-Matin	The Firm
Al-Wali	The Governor
Al-Hamid	The Praiseworthy
Al-Muhsi	The Appraiser
Al-Mubdi	The Conceiver
Al-Mu'id	The Restorer
Al-Muhyi	The Giver of Life
Al-Mumit	The Bringer of Death
Al-Hayy	The Ever-Living
Al-Qayyum	The Self-Subsisting One
Al-Wajid	The Finder
Al-Majid	The Illustrious
Al-Wahid	The Only One
Al-Ahad	The One
As-Samad	The Satisfier of Needs
Al-Qadir	The Powerful
Al-Muqtadir	The Omnipotent
Al-Muqaddim	The Expediter
Al-Mu'akhkhir	The Delayer
Al-Awwal	The First
Al-Akhir	The Last
Az-Zahir	The Manifest One

Al-Batin	The Hidden One
Al-Wali	The Friend
Al-Muta'ali	The Self-Exalted
Al-Barr	The Doer of Good
At-Tawwab	The Guide to Repentance
Al-Muntaqim	The Avenger
Al-Afuw	The Pardoner
Ar-Ra'uf	The Most Kind
Malik-al-Mulk	The King of Kings
Dhu-l-Jalal Wa-l-Ikram	The Lord of Majesty and Generosity
Al-Muqsit	The Equitable One
Al-Jami'	The Gatherer
Al-Ghani	The Rich One
Al-Mughni	The Enricher
Al-Mani'	The Preventer of Harm
Ad-Darr	The Distresser
An-Nafi	The Benefactor
An-Nur	The Light
Al-Hadi	The Guide
Al-Badi'	The Originator
Al-Baqi	The Everlasting One
Al-Warith	The Inheritor
Ar-Rashid	The Guide to the Right Path
As-Sabur	The Patient One

DISCIPLESHIP

◆

There is no doubt that Rumi's love for his spiritual teacher, Shams al-Din Muhammad ibn Ali, or Shams of Tabriz as he is more commonly known, was the source of inspiration for his celebrated verses of love and devotion. From the intensity of their mutual affection, Rumi poured forth an ocean of mystic poetry, including the most illustrious verses in the Persian language. Rumi composed almost a thousand poems mentioning or alluding to Shams of Tabriz.

O you, who are the doctor for our afflictions,
what are you prescribing for this pain exceeding all limits?
By God, even if you have a thousand concoctions,
I can't bear my life unless you reveal your face.

On the mystic path, a shaykh, or spiritual teacher, is considered essential for a spiritual seeker to develop, heal, and grow. For mystics, progress on the path is not possible without the loving guidance of a more illuminated soul. As Rumi wrote, "Do not entrust your hand except to the hand of a mystic master, for truth has become the hand-taker of that hand of his." The shaykh is a master in truth and love—an expert in drawing nearer to the divine. Sufi teachers are known to say: How can one become a lover alone?

O my life and my world—I've lost my life and my world!
O my moon, I've lost my earth and my sky!
Don't pour wine into my hands—pour it into my mouth!
Because, from being drunk on you, I've lost the way
*   to my mouth.*

A Sufi master gently guides a disciple through the process of purifying the heart to relinquish his ego and its desires and taste union with the divine presence. As Rumi writes: "A shaykh is a ladder to heaven." The loving hearts of these wise surgeons of the heart initiate a spiritual seeker into a spiritual chain of transmission from heart to heart that reaches back to the Prophet Muhammad and unlocks the treasure in a dervish's own heart.

I will become one hundred steps beyond reason.
I will become free from the existence of good and evil.
I am beyond goodness and the veil.
O you clueless ones: I will become the lover of my own self.

In the shadow of a shaykh, a dervish can move beyond rational thinking and the trappings of a heavenly reward or eternal damnation to encounter her own true inner essence. Attachment to both this world and the next must be abandoned on the mystic path. A dervish does not chase after material rewards on earth nor the promise of heavenly paradise in the hereafter. And anyway, as Rumi notes, "Hell is weakened and extinguished by the fire of love." All that matters, for the mystic, is drawing nearer to God in the here and now.

Shams was Rumi's qibla of truth. The qibla is the direction that should be faced for the five daily prayers so that worshippers are facing the holy city of Mecca. The mihrab, or carved prayer niche in the wall of a mosque, signals the direction of the holy city of Mecca. For Rumi, Shams's spiritual mastery and loving heart pointed the way toward the beloved.

THE IMAM OF LOVE

O you, who are the imam of love,
say: "God is Great!" for you are drunk.
Shake your two hands—
abhor self-centered existence.

You were devoted to time,
so you made haste.
Now the prayer time has come.
Get up! Why aren't you making ablution?

In hope of the qibla of truth,
you carve a hundred qiblas.
In hope of that idol's love,
you worship a hundred idols.

Fly a little higher, O soul,
O obedient and enslaved soul!
For the moon is high above,
and the shadow is down below.

Don't knock on every door like a beggar.
Knock the ring on heaven's door,
for your arm is long.
Since the flagon of heaven made you like that,
become a stranger to the world
so you may be liberated from the self.

I say to you: "How are you?"
No one ever says to a soul without "how":
"How are you?"

Tonight you're drunk and ruined.
When tomorrow comes, you'll see
what wineskins you've torn open
and what glasses you've broken.

With every glass I have broken,
my trust was in you,
for you have mended
a hundred thousand kinds of breaks.

O hidden image-maker,
in the depths of your soul,
you have a thousand forms
except the moon
and the lady of the moon.

If you have stolen the ring,
a hundred throats you have opened.
If you have melted one heart,
a hundred hearts and souls you have given.

I have gone insane.
Everything I say is from madness.
Quick! Say: "Yes, yes,"
if you are intimate with the
primordial covenant.

For dervishes, the polished heart of a spiritual master is
the gateway to self-knowledge and the divine. As the living

embodiment of love, the master bathes each spiritual aspirant in unconditional love and understanding to help heal all past wounds and unhealthy habits. Through this overpowering love, the mystic can feel safe to let go of the defenses of his ego and the negative characteristics polluting his heart.

Free from anger, fear, disappointment, abandonment, and trauma, a dervish can instead dedicate her attention, breath, and life to love—loving the divine and serving all creation to please the divine. A Sufi master also instructs a dervish in the proper codes of Sufi behavior and well-defined rules of ethics. One aim of the mystic is to become so absorbed in her teacher that her self dissolves completely and she tastes the salvation of nonexistence.

> *In drunkenness, I said to my teacher:*
> *"Enlighten me on nonexistence and existence."*
> *He gave me an answer, and said: "Go,*
> *keep your afflictions far from others,*
> *and you'll be free."*

Rumi was already a respected jurist and religious teacher when he first met the wandering mystic Shams of Tabriz while passing by the inn where Shams was staying in Konya. Though Rumi had succeeded his father as "Sultan of Scholars," his conventional career took a major mystical detour as a result of his spiritual connection and relationship with Shams of Tabriz. It was Shams who dared Rumi to start living experientially what he had been preaching philosophically. Their close relationship became the spiritual template for an intimate relationship with God. Rumi believed that friendship with a spiritual mentor is ultimately superior to the benefits of solitary spiritual seclusion.

THE GODLY FRIEND

When you fall into despair because of loneliness,
you'll rise again like the sun in the shade of your friend.

Go quickly, and seek a friend of God,
because as you do, God becomes your friend.

One whose gaze is fixed on seclusion,
has in reality already learned
about it from a friend.

Seclude not from your friend but from strangers,
just as one wears a fur coat
not in spring but winter.

As a charismatic wandering dervish, Shams had met over the decades with Sufi communities and shaykhs in Mecca, Damascus, Baghdad, Aleppo, and many cities around Turkey. Shams was a professional Qur'an teacher and well-versed in Islamic law and philosophy. Shams grew up in eastern Azerbaijan in the glorious city of Tabriz, a flourishing medieval center of Persian arts and culture, which today is in the Islamic Republic of Iran. At that time, Tabriz was teeming with mystic masters who transmitted the way of love through the embodiment of heightened spiritual states and stations, instead of just reading and discussing mystical and philosophical texts.

My eyes are already enriched by kohl from Isfahan,
unless you'd like to bestow some kohl upon me
fashioned from the soil of Tabriz.

All majesty is for the king of spirits, Shams of Tabriz.
All existences before his eminence emerged
are trivial in comparison.

It was Shams who drew Rumi's heart into the ecstasy of devotional music, poetry, and whirling. Shams taught Rumi how to whirl in divine reverie and love. While Rumi's father had modeled for Rumi how to feel God's presence and divine love in his heart, it was Shams's ecstatic embodiment of love that inspired Rumi to dive fully into mysticism.

Since your face became my prayer direction, O dearest,
I have no awareness of the Ka'ba and no trace of the qibla.
Without your face, facing Mecca is not possible,
because that qibla is for the body,
and your qibla is for the soul.

In Rumi's imagination, Shams, in reflecting the beauty of the beloved, assumed the place of the qibla—the direction for prayer. The qibla directs the bodily prayer practice of Islam, whereas a shaykh guides the soul through the inner mystical dimensions of the religion. According to Rumi, the mystical dimension is essential to religious devotion. He even boldly suggests that in a heightened state of spiritual ecstasy, the outer world—including the most sacred site of Islam—can disappear completely.

The Ka'ba is the black-clothed cube shrine in Mecca, which Muslims believe was rebuilt at God's command by Abraham and Ishmael. In its eastern corner is the Black Stone set in a ring of silver, which pilgrims kiss, touch, or point to while on pilgrimage. For Rumi, praying toward Mecca was obligatory for the body, but gazing upon the face of Shams was prayer for the soul. Shams pointed Rumi's longing and loving heart toward the divine within.

HE IS MY

When I start over, he is my leader.
When I seek my heart, he is its beloved.

When I search for peace, he is my intercessor.
When I go to war, he is my dagger.

When I come to a gathering, he is the wine and sweets.
When I enter the rose garden, he is the narcissus.

When I go into a mine, he is the ruby and carnelian.
When I come into the sea, he is the pearl.

When I wander in the desert, he is the oasis.
When I fly to the heavens, he is the stars.

When I exercise patience, he is my heart.
When I burn with heartache, he is the censer.

When I enter battle in wartime,
he, as commander, controls the formation of the ranks.

When I go to a banquet for festivities,
he is the wine pourer, musician, and cup.

When I write letters to friends,
he is the paper, pen, and ink.

When I awaken, he is my new awareness.
When I fall asleep, he enters my dreams.

When I seek a verse for my poetry,
he stretches my mind for rhyme.

Whatever form you can imagine,
he stands above it—
like painter and pen.

No matter how much higher you look,
he is higher than that "higher" of yours.

Go and leave behind lectures and textbooks.
You'd be better off having him as your manual.

Now be silent, for all six directions are his light.
And when you pass beyond the six directions,
he is the ruler.

O love, your satisfaction is my satisfaction—
this is what's most effective.

And your secret is my secret—
therefore, I won't reveal it.

Bravo, Shams of Tabriz,
who is shining like the sun,
and deeply worthy of himself.

Rumi and his teacher, Shams, retreated together in seclusion for long stretches to indulge in spiritual companionship, meditation, and ecstatic whirling far removed from the envious, suspicious, and judgmental eyes of others. Shams wrote, "They say that

I am a saint. I said, 'OK, let it be so, but what happiness does it bring to me?' If I were to be proud of it, it would be very ugly; but Mevlana, if one looks at the attributes defined by the Qur'an and the sayings of the Prophet, is a saint. And I am the saint of the saint, the friend of the friend; therefore I am less easily shaken, more firm."[1] As these two great mystic hearts gazed together into the divine mirror, it was impossible to know who was the disciple and who was the master. If Shams was the sun, was Rumi then the moon?

WHAT MAY I LEARN?

What may I learn in union with you?
What may I learn in separation from you?

Either you will be mixed in union with my pain,
or I will learn the cure from you in separation.

You will flee from me, saying:
"I don't know."
Or you will associate with me—
or, I will learn.

Before this, I feigned disdain and anger,
so I could learn in separation from you.

Since God is with you night and day,
after this, I will learn from God.

During my separation from you,
I found my punishment and reward.

From finding my own justice,
I will learn what justice is.

I will sweep the dust from your feet into my hands,
so I may learn alchemy from it.

I will become a speck of your sunlight,
so I may learn the meaning of Al-Duha:
"By the morning sunlight."

For your amber, I will become straw,
so I may feel the pull of amber.

I will close my two eyes to the two worlds—
this I will learn from the Prophet.

How may I learn the secret of the holy verse:
"He did not swerve or turn away,"
except from him?

In the sky,
I will circumambulate,
so I may learn yearning passion
from the whirling heavens.

I will break down the bonds of existence,
so I may learn to be like the moon—
without a robe.

Like a fish,
I will fashion an armor of scales for myself
so I may learn to swim in the ocean.

Like the heart,
I will drink blood,
so I may learn to travel and ascend
without hands and feet.

As no one's a total master in faithfulness,
I will learn faithfulness
from faithfulness itself.

The conclusion is this:
you are my beautiful face.
From you, I will receive
a cheerful countenance.

When Shams journeyed abruptly to Syria to give his intense spiritual relationship with Rumi a respite from the community's prying and jealous eyes, Rumi was plunged deep into despair. For Rumi, the separation was almost too much to bear: after all, the deeper a mystical bond is between spiritual companions, the harder it is to be apart. Shams, however, claimed not to suffer from the loss of their attachment; the distance did not cause him suffering, nor was being in Rumi's company the fountain of his happiness. His happiness, he claimed, came from within, and thus he was not dependent on any other person or circumstance.

Know that the way of pleasure is from within,
    not from without.
And it's folly to seek palaces and castles.

One man is drunk with happiness in the corner of a mosque,
while another is morose and aimless in a garden.

The palace is nothing—ruin your body!
The treasure is in the ruins, O my prince!

Don't you see that the drunk at the wine-feast
becomes happy when he's ruined?

Although the house is full of images, demolish it.
Seek the treasure and from the treasure—rebuild it.

In Rumi's poetry, he captures his longing to please his beloved Shams. A dervish's fear of being separated from his master physically or by rebuke or inattention could be even greater than his fear of hell.

Your wound is better than the medicine of others.
Your restraint is better than the giving of others.
Your cruelty is better than the loyalty of others.
And your cursing is better than the praise of others.

Rumi does not mean that Shams was cruel or abusive—rather, he is romanticizing his bittersweet dread of separation from the source of his love. In Rumi's time, the notion of shaykhhood and discipleship did not yet include the idea that a shaykh had authority over his disciples or any expectations of submission—the hierarchies and institutionalized orders that developed later were a different breed. Then, as well as now, Sufi masters treated their disciples leniently and let them make exemptions in their ascetic and ritual practices.

LEAVE ME BE

Go, lay your head on a pillow—leave me alone.
Leave me ruined, night-wandering, and suffering as I am.

From night until morning,
a wave of passion and I are alone.
If you want, come and absolve me.
Or, if you want, go away and be cruel.

Escape from me,
and you won't fall into misfortune, too.
Choose the path of health—
abandon this path of affliction.

My tears and I crept into the corner of heartache.
You could turn a watermill one hundred times
with my tears.

I have a tyrant with a heart like granite.
He could slaughter me, and no one would say to him:
"Prepare to pay the blood-money."

To the king of the lovely ones,
faithfulness is not obligatory.
O sallow-faced lover,
be patient and faithful.

This is a pain with no remedy
other than death.
So how should I say:
"Cure this pain?"

Last night in a dream,
I saw a shaykh in the quarter of love.
With his hand, he beckoned to me:
"Set out toward me."

If a dragon is on the path,
love is like an emerald.
From the splendor of this emerald,
drive away the dragon.

Enough—for I am beside myself.
But if you consider yourself a master of knowledge,
tell the glorious history of Ibn Sina,
and admonish the skeptic al-Ma'arri.

Shams defined himself as a "stranger": he did not feel attached to this world, nor did he identify with it. Further, Shams insisted that he was not interested in being a "debater": he was not interested in parsing the finer points of Islamic jurisprudence or policing acceptable boundaries and practices of mysticism. Instead, he was a foreigner to the world with his heart firmly tethered to the invisible realm. His whole consciousness was focused on loving the beloved.

Similarly, Rumi cast himself as a "mirror" instead of a "debater." A dervish, after all, is just "passing through" this world on the caravan of love heading back to its source. As Rumi wrote, "We never really came. This is just our shadow."

If shame is what you must have from this and that,
then you must bury the faults of others deep in the earth.
And if you mirror both good and bad,
then an outlook like a polished mirror you should have.

The heart of Shams was the mirror Rumi needed to see the beauty of his own essence. A shaykh, after all, helps a dervish challenge her ego and attachment to the self. As Shams wrote:

Let me give you the mirror, but if you see some fault on its face, do not blame the mirror, but something reflected onto the mirror. Know that it is your own image; find the fault in yourself!

In Rumi and Shams's day, mirrors were polished iron, and Rumi seized on this image to describe the polishing of a dervish's heart through encountering the pure heart of a spiritual master. As Shams stated, "The mirror is the truth, itself." Rumi also employed the image of the mirror to stress the importance of religious duties for polishing the heart and sharpening our rational faculties.

THE MIRROR OF THE HEART

So it was very well said by the permissive Prophet
that some rational thinking is better
*   than fasting and praying.*

For reason is your essence,
while prayers and fasting are accidental—
they became religious duties to complete the essence.
The intellect is like a mirror that is thereby burnished—
for piety paves the way to a pure heart.

Even if a mirror is basically corroded,
continuous polishing eventually revives it.
Never mind the mirror made of good material—
for which just a little polish will suffice.

In addition to the image of the mirror, Rumi imagined the human being as an astrolabe that is useless without a wise astronomer who knows how to use it. In the right hands, a dervish heart can be of service to the whole world. A dervish requires a spiritual master to reach her full potential and point the way to the heavens.

> *It's by the grace of God I've united with you,*
> *and been freed from the binding chains of separation.*
> *I've drunk so much wine of nonexistence,*
> *that I'm drunk from the day without beginning*
>   *to the day without end.*

Shams would take Rumi to socialize in the Armenian Christian and Jewish neighborhoods, including the tavern lanes—even though the Qur'an prohibits the drinking of wine. Rumi uses the image of "wine" in his poems as a symbol of the blessings of mystic love, the intoxication of ecstatic union, and the abandonment of overly rational thinking.

> *Look, O heart! Don't be deceived by every drunkenness.*
> *Jesus is drunk with truth, but his donkey is drunk with barley.*

Rumi's wine allusions follow a long tradition that stretches back to pre-Islamic Arabic poetry. Rumi distinguishes between the symbolic wine of mystical truth and regular wine.

> *That wine of truth—its seal is pure musk!*
> *As for regular wine, its conclusion is torment and stench.*

Rumi writes of the "wine of truth," the "wine of submission," the "wine of bliss," and the "wine of the free" in his descriptions of mystic love. The one who experiences such spiritual intoxication partakes in the delights of paradise on earth. For Rumi, his spiritual intoxication was stirred by Shams.

> *My drunkenness is from your existence,*
> *and your pleasant stream is my diving place.*

Rumi also alludes frequently to the "dregs" of wine—which are stronger than normal wine—to signal how excessively intoxicated he has become in his love of the divine. Just as there are different levels of drunkenness, so too are there different intensities of spiritual intoxication.

> *Deep thoughts and sorrow are nonexistent and unenduring*
> *where there is wine and rebab and kebab!*
> *Drink the eternal pleasure, O companions!*
> *As grass and flowers have done, place your lips on water's lips.*

Eternal pleasure is found when the spirit feasts on divine love, which has no beginning and no end. Rumi invites us to annihilate our sorrow and anxieties in the pleasures of mystic union. When we do so, our preoccupations with ourselves and the world are replaced with the sweet agony of yearning to be more intimate with the divine.

> *Tonight the agony of love is unceasing, unceasing!*
> *The goblet and the ruby wine are strong, strong!*
> *The blood of anguish and anxiety is halal, halal!*
> *While sleep and the longing for sleep are haram, haram.*

In Islam, something that is permitted is called "halal" in Arabic, while something that is forbidden is called "haram." For

Rumi, what is most pure is the pain of longing for nearness with the beloved. To take even a moment away from pursuing intimacy with the divine is akin to breaking Islamic law. When desire for closeness with the divine is sincere, we cannot escape its clutches—it is all-consuming.

> *The wine that for the people is prohibited—prohibited!*
> *Is for the soul of the wandering dervish continually flowing—*
> *   continually!*
> *Beware, O cupbearer, do not say: "It's finished—finished!"*
> *Where is our beginning and end? Where?*

Rumi frequently calls Sufis "drunkards" for being drunk with divine love. The tavern in his poetry symbolizes a dervish lodge or residence of a mystic master where thirsty hearts gather to get drunk on love. Shams clearly explains the difference between alcohol and the intoxication of mystic love:

> Why don't our friends take pleasure in that clean and infinite universe of ours? This universe embraces them and makes them drunk without ever making them aware of it. Everyone is in unanimous agreement that this universe is not a forbidden substance. Whereas wine is forbidden.[2]

Shams and Rumi were "wine worshippers"—ecstatic mystics intoxicated on divine love. While Shams did take Rumi to real taverns, along with Armenian churches and public baths, Rumi is insistent in his poetry that his wine is the libation of the spiritual realm. Along with his depictions of the tavern, a well-known symbol of the dervish lodge, Rumi paints the world as a public bathhouse to symbolize the temptations of the material realm and the sanctity that can be discovered in profane places.

This public bathhouse that is the home of genies,
is a place of retreat and rest for Satan.
But within it, a fairy-faced genie is hidden.
Thus, unbelief is where faith lies in wait to strike.

Rumi populates his poems with numerous landscapes of debauchery—public baths where temptations lurk, taverns where wine freely flows, ruins where vices are hidden, churches where Jesus is worshipped as God, and temples where Manichaean, Buddhist, and pagan idols are hung. In his day, these spaces were, in a sense, protosecular—divorced from the Islamic contexts in which Rumi was living and embedded. In these spaces of concealment and provocation, Rumi lets himself become liberated from the rigidity of religion and even piety itself.

DRUNK IN LOVE

The spirit that doesn't wear love as an inner garment—
its nonexistence is better than its existence,
for its existence is nothing but a shame.

Be drunk in love,
for love is everything that is.

Without the business and burden of love,
there is not a door to the beloved.

They ask: "What is love?"
Say: "To leave behind free will."
There's no free will for anyone
who hasn't been freed from free will.

The lover is a king of kings
with the two worlds strewn before him.
The king bestows no favors upon the scattering.

Love and the lover remain forever—
put nothing but this in your heart,
since all the rest won't last.

For how long can you embrace a dead lover—
instead, embrace the soul that can't ever be embraced!

That which spring begets will die in autumn.
But the flowers of the rose garden of love
don't need to wait for another spring to grow.

The rose from spring—
its friend is the thorn.
And the wine from crushed grapes
isn't without a hangover.

On this path, don't talk about looking ahead
   and expectations.
For by God, there isn't any worse death
than anticipation!

Brush aside the counterfeits,
if you aren't counterfeit yourself!
Open your ears to this point—
if you aren't already sporting a slave's earring.

Don't tremble on the horse of the body—
become lighter traveling on foot,

as God bestows wings to fly
on those not riding on the body.

Become liberated from anxiety—
completely simple-hearted,
like a mirror's face unmarred
by engravings and etchings.

When the mirror has become free of pictures,
all images are within it—
and that innocent-faced one isn't ashamed of any face.

Do you yourself want to be free of defect?
Then look to the one who isn't ashamed or afraid
of speaking the truth.

Since the iron-faced mirror acquired
    this art from purity,
imagine how much the face of the heart
    devoid of dust will gain!

I said: "What may it gain?"
No, I will not speak any further.
Silence is better—so the beloved won't say:
"He isn't a keeper of secrets."

MYSTIC DRUNKARDS

Go and tell that rebab player: "The drunkards are giving their
    greetings of peace to you!"
And tell the waterbird: "The drunkards are giving their
    greetings of peace to you!"

*And tell that prince of the cupbearers: "The drunkards are
    giving their greetings of peace to you!"*
*And tell that eternal life giver: "The drunkards are giving their
    greetings of peace to you!"*

*And tell that prince of ecstatic uproar: "The drunkards are
    giving their greetings of peace to you!"*
*And tell that provoker of passion and melancholy: "The
    drunkards are giving their greetings of peace to you!"*

*O you, whose beautiful face shames the moon: "The drunkards
    are giving their greetings of peace to you!"*
*And, O peace and quiet of the heart: "The drunkards are giving
    their greetings of peace to you!"*

*O soul of the soul! O soul of the soul: "The drunkards are giving
    their greetings of peace to you!"*

"But there is only one drunkard here!"

"The drunkards are giving their greetings of peace to you!"

*O desire of desires: "The drunkards are giving their greetings of
    peace to you!"*

Quick—take off that veil!

"The drunkards are giving their greetings of peace to you!"

A Sufi disciple tries to model the behavior of his spiritual
master to absorb the master's spiritual states and shed the trap-
pings of the ego. He carefully watches how the mystic teacher
conducts himself in each moment to better practice dervish

etiquette, enact virtue in daily life, and live in spiritual community. A disciple practices dissolving his self into the master to feel the peace of being unburdened from selfhood. Eventually, the spiritual master appears to speak through a disciple: the student begins to take on the essence of his teacher.

In the following verses, Rumi explores the imitative nature of the master-disciple relationship. Sufis contend that the mystic path rests upon spiritual knowledge inherited from the Prophet Muhammad that is transmitted from master to disciple—from heart to heart—through imitation. At first, the ecstasy and conduct of the dervish are but a reflection of those of the teacher—until they are transformed through spiritual alchemy into genuine expressions of love and devotion.

IMITATION AND COMPULSION

A disciple came into the room to be near his shaykh,
and found him weeping and crying out.

Seeing the shaykh weeping,
the disciple burst into tears,
and began weeping too.

When someone tells a joke among friends,
the one with the ability to listen laughs once,
but the one who's deaf laughs twice.

His first laugh is from imitation and compulsion,
upon seeing others in the group laughing.

So he laughs to be like the rest,
still unaware of why they're laughing.

Thus, he inquires as to the reason why.
When he finds out, he bursts into laughter again too.

So the imitating disciple is akin to a deaf person
in his mindless exultation.

He is a mere reflection of his shaykh—
the source of his light and overflowing joy.
So the spiritual ecstasy is not from the disciples,
but the master.

It is like water inside a basket in the river,
or a beam of light on glass.

It would be defective of them to assume
they own what's inside of them.

As the basket is taken out of the river,
the basket realizes the fine water inside it
belongs to the river.

Likewise, glass discovers from the sunset
that the beautiful, shining moon
is the true owner of its luminosity.

When the divine command: "Arise!" opens
a deaf man's eye of spiritual vision,
he will laugh yet again.

He will even laugh at his own laughter,
which first arose from imitation.

He will say: "By these roundabout and convoluted ways,
I thought this was reality and that was the mystery and secret.

How for so long did I rejoice
in blindness and zeal
in that valley of ignorance?

What was I imagining—
and what was the truth in reality?
My weak perception was producing an incomplete picture."

A novice on the way can't think in the same manner
as senior dervishes on the path,
for their imagination is far
from the righteous search for truth.

All infants think about is their nanny, milk,
*   raisins, and walnuts—*
and screaming and crying.
The imitating disciple is like a sick infant—
despite his nuanced discourse and skill in debate.
It's his knack for abstraction and proficiency in proofs
that drive him far from insight.

By fixating on intellectual details and debates,
he makes a waste of the intellect's beneficial quality—
kohl for his spiritual vision.

O you imitator! Come back from Bukhara
and hurry toward humility,
so you become brave enough to proceed on the path.

Then you will arrive in the Other Bukhara,
the grand assembly hall inside yourself,
where even the heroes of the way are novices.

Rumi paints the dervish as an infant in her imitation of her master's conduct, state, and knowledge. She is a reflection of the light of her mystic master—she does not "own" her spiritual states any more so than a basket floating on water owns the water inside of it or glass owns the light that shines through it! Rumi asks: Who, in reality, is the true ocean of love and the light of knowledge? Where is the source?

Eventually, a dervish heart becomes polished enough to reflect the light and love of the divine. The dervish strives to attain a state of perfection that imitates not only his spiritual teacher but God himself, as he attempts to adopt and embody the divine attributes as captured in the ninety-nine names of God. In time, a dervish may pass beyond intoxication and become the one who bestows intoxication. Mystic knowledge is attained through this experiential path—not through books and discourse.

In Rumi's poetry, he is often critical of scholars, judges, intellectuals, and philosophers who prize rational thinking as opposed to spiritual knowledge and insight. For centuries before Rumi's time, Bukhara (in present-day Uzbekistan) was a major center of Islamic learning, as well as a bustling producer of political, cultural, and economic power and influence. In the madrasas of Bukhara, theologians, philosophers, and scientists produced knowledge of many kinds. Rumi frequently invokes "Bukhara" in his poetry as a symbol of the pretentiousness and grandiose pride of rational knowledge. He warns dervishes not to be seduced by the allure of rational and prestigious knowledge. He critiques Bukhara's intellectual achievements and renown and instead urges dervishes to seek the "Other Bukhara"—inward, spiritual knowledge grounded in mystical truth and direct encounters with the divine.

* * *

Be patient in struggle and suffering,
so that moment to moment
you may see permanence in annihilation.

Every time Baba saw me get anxious during my retreat, he'd
say, *"Lazim sabr."* "Patience is necessary." This became the re-
frain of my retreat. For people in the West, patience, though it
may be considered a virtue, is hard to find. However, the mystic
path requires the patience of Job for a heart to ripen. In the
words of Rumi: "Patience is the key to tranquility."

Whenever Baba said *"Lazim sabr,"* I became more attuned to
how often I felt impatient. I became more aware that every mo-
ment requires patience—with both myself and others. My work
with Baba would be to embody patience, as a reflection of the
patience of the beloved—one of whose ninety-nine names is "The
Patient One." Memorizing the ninety-nine divine names in Ara-
bic was helping to distract and quiet my mind, while simultane-
ously expanding my consciousness of the different modes I could
choose to be in. To chart his own spiritual progress, Rumi, like
his father, kept a spiritual diary—so I decided to keep one, too.

Baba had been a model of patience himself in dealing with me
and my many lapses, such as my embarrassing habit of sleeping
in late and forgetting to make his breakfast. At the sound of his
gentle knock on my door, I'd bound from slumber in my pajamas,
cover my messy pillow hair with a bandana, and leap up the stairs
to boil his eggs in the Turkish coffee tin. No admonishment or
mention was necessary: the knock was enough.

The mystic path is a merciful and forgiving one. In fact,
some medieval dervish manuals even had special sections on
ethical and social dispensations—approved departures from
the usual dervish rules—which took into account the complex-
ities of daily life, the inescapability of human fallibility, and the

importance of mercy, forgiveness, and compassion. According to Rumi, a devout person's patience and serenity result from her trust in the divine. She seizes the blessings of the world in a peaceful manner because of her trust in God.

THE TRUE BELIEVER

*The true believer seizes the blessings of the world in a calm
and deliberate manner because of her trust in God the Alive.*

*She is safe from the loss of time and rival rebels,
since she knows the king's wrath over her enemies.*

*She is safe from her fellow servants of the Lord,
who could trouble her and gain the advantage.*

*The true believer has seen the king's justice
in managing his retinue,
which prevents injustice being inflicted
by one servant upon another.*

*Consequently, she doesn't hurry and remains tranquil,
confident in not losing the source of her joy.*

*Endowed with serenity, patience, and radical acceptance,
she is content, compassionate, and pure of heart.*

*Her serenity is from the compassionate, divine light cast upon her,
whereas haste is triggered by the devil's temptations.*

*For one scared by the devils of poverty and scarcity
is prone to lay down the burdensome load of patience.*

SELF-DISCIPLINE

◆

Self-discipline in the Sufi sense does not refer to modern worldly forms of discipline, like dieting or exercise. Rather, self-discipline in the mystic sense means the disciplining of the ego and the intentional practice of proper Sufi conduct. Rumi wrote: "The mother of idols is the idol of your self." Committed to relentless self-examination, Sufis practice constant vigilance to keep the desires of their egos in check and uphold high moral and ethical standards at all times.

Self-discipline in Rumi's day required practice in abstaining from the desires of the body, such as food and sleep, as well as turning away from ambitious worldly desires for a good reputation, money, and fame. Today, as in the past, dervishes try to refrain from speaking badly of others or envying what others possess.

> *Pouring envy and greed from love's open sea*
> *and the waters of bliss,*
> *we steal happiness from each other.*
> *No fish ever hoards water.*
> *Without the sea, there's no existence.*

Swimming in the ocean of love and oneness of being, how can there be any place for envy or greed? Love is our very essence and the true nature of reality—we are immersed in it. When hearts drown in love, they unite in bliss and their shared humanity.

Rumi himself was well trained and well practiced in asceticism.

In his poems, Rumi encourages the reader to abstain from eating excess food and partaking in idle or harmful speech; he cautions his readers to choose their words wisely. A preoccupation for Rumi, as well as for al-Ghazali before him, was the question of gluttony. Sufi brotherhoods in medieval times had many manners related to eating, acceptable meal conversation, hospitality, and the serving of food.

Like his father, Rumi was particularly fond of the virtues and benefits of fasting for a month at a time to help tame his ego and deepen his meditative states. Even as a young child, Rumi would fast for several days. In his diary, Rumi mentions the rewards of fasting, and in his poetry, he sings its praises. Of course, eating is also a metaphor for excessive desire and lust.

LUST

Lust arises from too much eating.
So either eat less or get married
to escape from this vice.

When you eat too much, you're vulnerable to sin,
just like when you earn an income—
and have spending money for lewd things.

But marriage acts like the expression:
"There is no power or strength except by God,"
in warding off the afflictions
the devil casts upon you

So if you're voracious, get married at once,
otherwise the lecherous cat
will come and snatch the tail fat.

When a donkey is jumping and kicking,
it's swiftly loaded with stones
before agitation consumes him.

Stay away from the fire,
if you're unfamiliar with what it does.
Don't approach the fire with your limited knowledge.

Without sufficient knowledge of the fire and pot,
neither the pot nor the soup are spared from the flames!

For the pot to work well and food to cook properly,
you don't need just boiling water—
but culinary expertise and artistry too.

In Islam, fasting is a form of self-denial used to transcend the needs and desires of the body and to retreat into the soul. In medieval times, some criticized Sufis who abstained from food for long stretches and isolated themselves on long retreats as excessively ascetic. Such critics also endorsed communal travel over solitary wandering to make self-starvation more difficult to pull off. Today, outside of the obligatory fasting of Ramadan, most dervishes do not engage in long fasts or extended periods of retreat, although some committed dervishes and spiritual masters are known to do so.

Fasting from the temptations of the world and indulgences of the self helps a dervish progress on the spiritual path. As Rumi writes: "The world's appearance is a paradise, but in reality it is a hell. It is a viper full of venom, though its facade is a rose-cheeked beauty." Rumi recommends changing one's diet from a gluttonous love of food and other ephemeral pleasures to feasting on the spiritual food that is obtained through fasting from the temptations of the world. When we abstain from the excessive pleasures of the world, he contends, we do not lose—but gain.

THE PATHWAY OF SALVATION

The devil is so in love with the world that
　　he goes deaf and blind.
Such a love is only superseded
　　by another love as abiding.

When he tastes wine from the cellar of certainty,
he gradually moves on to find an alternative love.

Hey you, voracious fool! This is how you should
　　elevate yourself—
the only method is to change your diet.

Hey you, heartsick one! Rise toward the cure—
the entire regimen is to change your temperament.

Hey you, imprisoned by your addiction to food—
you'll be bailed out if you can bear to wean yourself off.

Truly, there's an abundance of food in starvation—
so look for it and keep up your hopes, you shunner!

Be like an open eye and feed yourself with light,
complying with the angels.

O you, the best of humanity!
Make the adoration of truth your diet,
as an angel would do,
to deliver yourself from suffering.

If the angel Gabriel doesn't find his food in corpses,
it doesn't mean he's inferior to a vulture
when it comes to strength.

Look, what a blessed table is spread in the world!
But it is hidden from the eyes of the vile.

Even if the whole world became a garden of riches,
people with the temperament of a mouse or snake
would still feast on dirt.

While Rumi wrote about the blessings of fasting in his poems, he also wrote about the joys of breaking the fast. The eid, or holiday, in the following poem refers to Eid al-Fitr, the three-day holiday feast of "breaking" the monthlong fast of Ramadan.

HOLIDAY BLESSINGS

May the Eid be blessed for the lovers!
O lovers! May your Eid be blessed!

The Eid has the scent of our soul,
may it be blessed in the world like our soul!

To you, O moon of the earth and the heavens,
may it be blessed up to the first heavens!

The Eid has come!
The sign of union is visible.
O lovers! May this sign be blessed!

Don't break the Ramadan fast
except on his sugary lips.
May his sugar be a blessing for your mouth!

The Eid wrote on the edge of his lips:
"May this wine be blessed without limit!"

The Eid has come!
O pure soul,
may your heavy wine goblets be blessed!

How long will you drink in secret,
O Salahuddin, my spiritual companion!
May your hidden kisses be blessed!

If you give a drop to me,
I will say:
"May it be blessed for me and whoever you say!"

Despite his elite status in Konya, Rumi was not interested in sumptuous feasts, even if served on an imperial table. There was no "pride" to be taken in such delicacies and indulgences. Rumi especially treasured the observance of Ramadan, the blessed holy month of fasting from dawn until dusk, and he penned a number of verses extolling its blessings.

The wheel of heaven can't contain the one
who's become your famished lover.

Life is the servant of the one who became your servant.
Biting my fingernails, I came in through your door—
but I went out snapping my fingers after being at your side.

Rumi aimed to be a "starved" one—not just a dervish devoted to fasting, but a dervish who fasts from worship of the self and the temptations of the world. He also abstained as much as he could from sleep to devote himself to praying throughout the night. The wheel of heaven that Rumi mentions in many of his poems is invoked as a wheel of fortune that is under the control of the divine. On top of that, the wheeling sky is constantly revolving—with the heavens whirling around us day and night!

The lover revolves around the dew and the springtime,
while the ascetic is preoccupied with prayer beads
   and prostrations.
The ascetic is entangled in thoughts of bread,
while the lover longs for the water's edge.
The lover thirsts, while the ascetic worries about his hunger.

As much as Rumi was devoted to fasting to purify his mind and soul, he also juxtaposed the ascetic with the ecstatic lover of the divine. The ascetic denies herself pleasure and takes refuge in self-denial practices and rituals, while the lover is thirsting to drink in the pleasures of divine love. Ascetics focused on denying the self are still preoccupied with the self, whereas the true lover is attached only to thoughts of the beloved.

Cast out greed, jealousy, and hatred from your heart!
Recast bad habits and mistrust.

Denial is to your detriment—go lessen it!
Avowal benefits you—so increase it!

In the struggle to rid the heart of negative characteristics, Rumi downplays self-denial in favor of divine affirmation. Affirm the divine transcendent reality, he urges! Affirming virtue leads to altruism, while denying virtue leads to destruction. Instead of being fixated on disciplining the self, Rumi suggests deepening one's gaze on the beloved for the ultimate transformative benefit and power of love.

Medieval dervish manuals stress the importance of sincerity, which Rumi highly prized as well. Service, if not done with sincerity, is nothing but worship of the self. Rumi critiques such religious hypocrisy in his poems. For Rumi, the religious obligations of Islam, such as charity, had to be performed with sincerity—otherwise they were useless. Thus, it was not enough to merely go through the motions of prayer, fasting, giving alms, or pilgrimage: one had to have a sincere intention and loving connection to the divine in performing these acts.

SINCERITY OF PRACTICE

Prayer, fasting, pilgrimage, and jihad
are testimonies of belief.

While charity, almsgiving, and abandoning envy
testify to your inner secret.

When you offer hospitality and food to a guest,
it's a way to express being in harmony with them.

Just like gifts, presents, and offerings
bear witness to your pleasure with them.

Why does someone donate: to be crafty or sincere?
They want to show they have an inner gem.

Fasting and charity bear witness
to the hidden jewels of piety and generosity.

Fasting tells of one's piety:
"He has abstained from halal food—
so naturally he distances himself from haram food too!"

And charity speaks of generosity: "He doesn't need to steal
*   money,*
since he's giving away from his own savings."

But if they're crafty in their practice,
these two testimonies are rejected at the trial of Divine Justice.

For if they're donating seeds, not out of mercy and benevolence,
but as bait to hunt—then they're only acting as hunters!

In his fasting, the deceitful person is like a cat
who plays possum to effortlessly seize the prey.

Such deviated practice has caused distrust
toward religion in countless hearts—
and given a bad name to believers
who sincerely fast and generously give.

Sufis have long been associated with charity and helping those
most in need. Poor people, the mentally unwell, and travelers in
need of lodging have always found refuge in Sufi communities

around the world—in the past and the present. The generosity of Sufis on the peripheries of empires—in feeding the poor and tending to those in material and spiritual need—helped Islam spread in many regions of the world. Helping those in need is seen by Sufis as one of the best ways to remedy self-preoccupation and be of service to humanity. After all, it is one's sincere and selfless deeds that demonstrate the true inner state of a mystic's soul.

SPIRITUAL EXAMINATION

Words and deeds are witnesses to one's consciousness,
from which you can infer one's inner state.

When you lack access to the secret of someone's inner-self,
you should observe its outward manifestations,
like diagnosing an illness from a sick person's urine.

The word and deed are like a sick person's urine
taken by the doctor of the body as evidence.

Likewise, the physician of the spirit peers into the soul,
and in the spiritual way assesses one's faith.

Physicians of the spirit have no need
to examine the word and deed.
So watch out for them, for they are spies of the heart.

The testimonial of the word and deed only works
in the case of a person detached from their origin,
like a stream that has not yet reached the sea.

* * *

Everywhere I am, I am present at your dinner table.
I am your guest, your guest, your guest!

"Dinner is served," said Mehmet, a hipster filmmaker with retro black-rimmed thick glasses and a fitted rugby striped shirt.

The dervishes put out their cigarettes and filtered inside to take their places at the low round table, where Baba reached for the large wooden ladle to scoop a mound of vegetables and meat into my bowl from the large communal pot.

"Eat," he said forcefully, triggering flashbacks to the summer before my senior year of college when I was forced into an eating disorder program. While I didn't feel as acutely anorexic as I'd once been, my appetite was still depressed.

"Thank you—not too much," I said, patting my belly as if I were full. Baba's response was to load even more food onto my plate.

Noticing that I wasn't able to eat more than a few extra bites, he stabbed a piece of chicken with his fork, and turned to me slowly.

"Here, eat this," he said, and slid the fork into my mouth. Little did I know that this unexpected act was a time-honored Sufi tradition—the transmission of love through feeding and being fed like a child.

"You don't eat enough," Baba said, before dropping the fork and turning toward the door to greet the dervishes who were arriving late.

There was clearly no use in hiding my defects from Baba—he was able to read each miserable corner of my psyche for himself. To pretend I didn't have any problems would have been a waste of time.

After the meal, as Baba reached for his after-dinner cigarette, I lunged to grab his lighter before the other dervishes could, since he encouraged us to compete in acts of service.

Above all else, a Sufi must be a loving servant—to the divine and all creation. For a Sufi, every moment is an opportunity to serve. In this sense, a Sufi is a servant of the moment itself—ready to serve in whatever way the moment calls for.

Service is a prime way to work on annihilating the ego, but service is not done in service of the ego: good acts are not carried out to appear "good" or "pious" to others or to win points or favor with one's shaykh. Sufis see service as an act of love. If one is in a constant state of love, serving others comes naturally.

To practice how to serve from a place of love instead of ego, Baba had me and the other dervishes practice giving him a glass of water over and over again. One at a time, we would stand at the door with a glass of water on a tray and a napkin folded on our shoulder. We would bow to him for permission to enter the room, and then kneel on our right knee before him. After kissing the glass, we would raise it slightly to our forehead as a form of respect, and then offer him the water. The trick was to do it without ego or selfhood—to practice offering the glass as an act of love and gesture of oneness instead of an object offered from one individual to another.

Being the one to serve Baba's food or light his cigarette, however, was not meant to instill pride as his "favorite." On the contrary, as we sought out countless opportunities for service, we were constantly in a state of looking outside of ourselves, begging to be of help—instead of being preoccupied with our own anxieties, fears, and concerns. Our peace of mind was found in helping others.

Having been compulsively driven my whole life (I finished five

Ivy League degrees and a postdoctoral fellowship at Harvard by age thirty), I welcomed the subversion of my competitive instincts: competing in good works and service made me more attentive to the needs of "the other" rather than to my own insecurities.

Feeling a bit precocious, one night I placed a sugar cube between my pointer finger and thumb, and turned toward Baba.

"This is how the dervish annihilates himself in love," I said, dropping the sugar cube into my tea—the specks of sugar dissolving instantly. With a sly smile, Baba sipped his Turkish coffee.

"Tell me, how much do you love love?" Baba said, raising his eyebrows to prompt an answer out of me.

"Well, there's nothing but love, so—so how could I love anything other than love?" I said. Baba wasn't impressed.

"Tell me, how much do you love love?" he asked again, with more intensity, as if his tone might help me solve this Sufi riddle.

"It is love itself that loves love," I replied, taking myself out of the equation. After all, the only true reality for a Sufi is total absorption in love.

I thought of a story told by one of Rumi's favorite poets, the Persian mystic Attar, about a madman in chains whispering a secret to God. When someone put an ear to his lips to discover the secret of his heart, the person heard him saying to God, "This madman of Yours had for a time shared a house with You. But there was no room for You and me, for either You had to be in the house or I. And so by your command I have left this house: since You are here—I, madman that I am, have gone."

"How much do you love love?" Baba asked again, seemingly exasperated. Failing to provide an adequate answer of my own, I tried quoting Rumi.

"When I come to love, I am ashamed of all I have ever said

about love," I said. Baba gave up. He took a long deliberate sip
of his coffee, and then changed the subject. I didn't know if I
had passed the test or failed. What was the answer he had been
looking for? And what was the answer lying buried deep in my
own heart?

DYING LIKE SUGAR

Lovers who die with awareness
die like sugar in the presence of the beloved.

In primordial time,
they drank the water of life,
so they don't die in the way others do.

Since their souls have congregated in love,
they don't die like other people in the crowd.

They've passed beyond the angels to divine grace.
They're far from dying like ordinary humans.

Do you assume that lions too die
outside the gate like dogs?

When lovers die in their journey,
the soul's king sprints to greet them.

When they die at the feet of that moon,
they all shine like the sun.

The lovers who are each other's soul
all die in their love for one another.

For all of them, the water of love soothes
  their aching livers—
all of them come and die in that heartache.

Each one is like a unique pearl—
they do not die at the side of their mothers and fathers.

Lovers fly to the heights of the heavens,
while deniers die in the pits of hell.

Lovers open the eye of the unseen—
the rest all die deaf and blind.

And lovers who never sleep at night out of fear,
all die without dread or danger.

But those who worshipped fodder here—
they were cows and die like donkeys.

While those who sought spiritual vision,
die happy and smiling at the unveiled revelation.

The king of kings places them next to his gentle grace—
they do not die like cattle,
wretched and trapped in a pen.

Those who seek to emulate and embody
the virtues, morality, and manners of the Prophet Muhammad,
die like Abu Bakr and 'Umar.
Annihilation and death are far from them.
And yet I have recited this poem,
supposing they could die.

VIRTUE

◆

Being a dervish is being in touch with one's full self—the good and the bad. A dervish must know herself to know the divine. To do so, she must embark on the path of humility—in facing her faults and cleansing her heart of negative qualities. A dervish knows that she is not perfect; she does not hide her imperfections to pass as pious or attract praise. As Rumi wrote, "Good and evil are part of the dervish. Whoever is not like this, she is not a dervish."

> *To my heart I said: Don't be better than others.*
> *Go and be a balm of kindness—don't be one resembling a sting.*
> *If you want nothing bad to reach you from anyone,*
> *don't be one who speaks evil, associates with evil,*
>   *and thinks evil.*

Sufis place a high importance on practicing the virtues of love, contentment, gratitude, and patience. They also seek to perfect intention, sincerity, and truthfulness. Dervishes cultivate virtue, cleanse the heart of imperfections, and refine the soul as if they are always in the presence of the divine—because in their heart, they always are.

> *The owner of the heavens knows your secrets,*
> *for he knows them hair by hair and vein by vein.*
> *I guess you may deceive people with hypocrisy,*

but how will you be with him who knows
everything through and through?

The mystic philosopher al-Ghazali praised the Sufis for their outstanding ethical conduct and wisdom. After exhaustively contemplating and researching different sects and practices of Islam, along with other religions, he concluded:

> I knew with certainty that the Sufis are those who uniquely follow the way to God Most High, their mode of life is the best of all, their way the most direct of ways, and their ethic the purest. Indeed, were one to combine the insight of the intellectuals, the wisdom of the wise, and the lore of scholars versed in the mysteries of revelation in order to change a single item of Sufi conduct and ethic and to replace it with something better, no way to do so would be found! For all their motions and quiescences, exterior and interior, are learned from the light of the niche of prophecy.

For al-Ghazali, the virtuous and ethical conduct of the Sufis flowed from the light of prophecy shining through the hearts of all the prophets mentioned in the Qur'an. For Sufis, the Prophet Muhammad serves as their specific template for human ethical perfection and the model for virtuous conduct. A Sufi looks for guidance too in their own heart and soul.

When you are conscious of doing good,
you gain a new lease on life and ease.
But when a fault or evil deed emerges,
that vitality and tranquility vanish.

The cultivation of good virtue is a basic tenet of the mystic path. A Sufi aims to become a perfected person. Muslim mystics are known for their virtuous action and saintly piety. This is the work of grace but continual practice. However, Rumi notes that the mystic path is not laborious: "What is required is self-surrender, not long and arduous work." Rumi's teacher, Shams, describes the saintly conduct of a dervish:

> He is the kind of person before whom human beings and angels put their ladders down in admiration of his qualities and words. Acrobats who astonish people with their rope skills are amazed at the length and strength of his rope, and by the fearlessness and heroism of his feats. Hearts leap at the sight of his miracles.[3]

While Rumi emphasizes "purity" in many of his poems, this does not mean that he did not joke or trade the occasional insult in his poetry and life. In his poetry, he incorporates bawdy humor, and in his life, like anyone, he could unleash an insult. After all, sometimes a teacher has to be crass to make a point: "If you aren't a donkey's ass, look exclusively at the garden."

SHAME

Let there be shame on the people of the world—shame!
A bunch of stupid, pathetic fakes!

Appearing outwardly as ascetics,
while their inner abode is in shambles!

For two farthings one can buy
three or four assloads of these idiots!

Rumi was especially taken as a boy with Persian animal fables that told moral tales. As a result, his poetry is populated with a menagerie of animals who impart moral and spiritual lessons to encourage the cultivation of virtue and inspire transcendence of the self and the material world. Rumi imagined the development of a mystic as a progression from a nightingale to a falcon on the hunt for deep mystical truths. A mystic is always on a relentless quest to understand and perceive reality.

> *What is the soul? The soul is conscious of good and evil—it*
> *rejoices in the face of kindness,*
> *and weeps in the face of injury.*

In Rumi's *Masnavi,* he devotes over a thousand lines to present a parable of sorts about four birds whose vices demonstrate the importance of virtuous conduct. Rumi was especially influenced and inspired by Attar's *Conference of the Birds*, a masterpiece of Persian literature in which the birds of the world, plagued with destructive fears and doubts, seek a king to lead them. The wise hoopoe guides them to choose the simurgh as their king. The entire work is an allegory of the mystic path: the insecurities of a spiritual seeker, the benefits of spiritual community, and the necessity for wise guidance to ascend to the divine realm.

Rumi drew inspiration for the passages below from his father's commentary on a portion of the Qur'an in which God uses four birds to show Abraham that he can resurrect the dead. As Rumi explains in his masterpiece: the duck represents greed; the rooster, lust; the peacock, pride; and the crow, attachment to the temptations of this world.

INTRODUCTION OF THE FOUR BIRDS

> *This body has become a seat for the four temperaments,*
> *which are named after the four mischievous birds.*

If you wish people an eternal life,
then behead these four ill-fated, evil birds.

Revive them into another kind of being,
so no harm will come from them again.

The four spiritually deceitful birds
have made a home in the hearts of the people.

Since you are the prince of all the righteous hearts
in this round, O you,

the Caliph of Truth,

behead these four living birds—
make the unenduring people everlasting.

The duck, the peacock, the crow, and the rooster—
these are examples of the four dispositions in the soul.
The duck is greed, and the rooster is lust.
The peacock is vainglory, and the crow is worldly desire.

The object of the crow's desire is this:
his hope and hunger for immortality or a long life.

THE DUCK'S BILL

It is due to greed that the duck's bill
is always jammed in the ground,
no matter how wet or dry,
searching endlessly for buried treasure.

Its throat isn't idle for even a second—
and it heeds no command other than: "Eat!"

The duck is like a looter who digs a hole
to sneak into a house and hastily fill his sack.

He crams whatever's at hand in his bag,
whether noble or wretched,
be it pearls or chickpeas.

Lest another rebel arrive who could surpass him in looting,
he shoves everything in the sack,
no matter wet or dry.

Dreading his tight time and narrow window of opportunity,
he grabs the sack as fast as possible to flee.

He does not trust that his sultan
would not permit any rebel to confront him.

THE PRETENTIOUS PEACOCK

We come now to the deceptive peacock
who shows off to make its name and brand.

The peacock strives to catch people's attention,
not knowing or caring if they're good or bad—
ignorant of the consequences and use of its actions.

In being oblivious, the peacock is like a trap for prey,
as a trap doesn't know the purpose or result of its job.

What does a trap get or lose from the catch?
I'm in total bewilderment from its futile game!

THE CAW OF THE CROW

There seems to be no end to this discourse!
And now, if we asked Abraham:
"O friend of God, why did you kill the crow?"

He would respond: "Due to the divine command."
But what was the rationale behind the command?
We shall now reveal some of the secrets behind it.

The black crow constantly caws and cries for continuity,
demanding a long life in this world.

It is like Iblis, the devil, who requested from God—
the Pure and Incomparable—
the extension of his corporeal life until the Resurrection.

Iblis said: "Give me reprieve until the Day of Judgment."
Would that he had said:
"We repent, our Lord!"

Life without repentance is all agony of spirit:
Being absent from God is instant death.

Life and death—both of these are beautiful when conscious of God.
Without God, the water of life is fire.

Furthermore, it was from the effect of the divine curse—
when God cast the devil out of heaven—
that Iblis was demanding a long life in such a presence.

To desire anything other than God is the assumption of gain,
but it is entirely loss!

And to especially crave a life drowned in estrangement from
   God—
is to behave like a fox in the presence of a lion, pleading:
"Give me longer life so I may go farther back—
grant me more time so I may become less."

As a result, he becomes a mark for the divine curse:
Evil is the one who seeks to be damned.

The good life is to nourish the spirit in nearness to God.
The crow's life is for the sake of eating shit.

The crow says: "Give me more life so that I can eat more shit.
Give me this always for I am evil-natured."

Were that foulmouthed one not a shit-eater,
he would say:
"Deliver me from the nature of the crow!"

THE ROOSTER

Why am I being so talkative like the ill-fated crow?
Abraham, you tell us why you killed the rooster!

"Because of the divine command," he replied.
"Then tell me the wisdom behind the command,
so I can understand it literally with full-fledged precision."

The rooster is lustful and very lecherous—
it is drunk on that poisonous and flavorless wine.

* * *

I am the lover of love, and love is my lover too.
The body has become the lover of the soul,
and the soul the lover of the body.

"Hafiz, it's time to teach Zemzem how to make Turkish coffee," Baba said, feeding me a piece of baklava from his fork after a feast one night.

Throughout the centuries in the Mevlevi Sufi Order, each dervish has traditionally been assigned a role in the Sufi lodge. One dervish is responsible for serving the tea and coffee, another is in charge of cooking, and yet another is the arranger of the shoes at the door. And on and on! Everyone has a role in which to practice service.

Baba explained that coffee has held a special importance for Sufis since its very beginning. Coffee, called the wine of Islam, traces its heritage to a medieval Sufi shaykh working in Ethiopia, who brought coffee beans from Africa to Yemen. From Yemen, coffee found its way to the streets of Istanbul, where the brew helped Sufis stay awake for their long nighttime whirling ceremonies and divine remembrance meditations. In fact, in Turkey there were originally religious decrees issued against coffee, as it was first seen as a drug.

"Allons-y," Hafiz said. "Let's go." Since Hafiz, respected for being the daily guardian of a sultan's tomb, had studied in France for many years, we enjoyed conversing together in French—since my French was markedly better than my Turkish.

What spiritual lesson, I wondered, was I supposed to learn from brewing Turkish coffee?

Hafiz and I rose, bowed with our hands over our hearts, and retreated to the kitchen, where he grabbed the tin of finely ground coffee from the windowsill.

"Have you ever made Turkish coffee before?" he asked.

"No," I replied.

I hadn't made much of anything at all. Hafiz could tell I wasn't in my element. I was a jack of many trades, but cooking was not one of them.

"It's imperative that you watch carefully and remember exactly what I do. I will show you this only once, and then it will be your responsibility," he said, as he began to pour grinds into the tin vessel I used to boil eggs every morning for Baba.

To match his seriousness, I squinted my eyes and took a deep breath to concentrate. Though my eyes darted around the room frantically for a notebook and pen, they found none in sight. Hafiz quizzed me at each step.

"How many scoops of coffee did I put in there?" he said, adding water.

"Three," I said.

Next, Hafiz placed a surprisingly large number of sugar cubes into the concoction—twelve to be exact.

"Now, watch carefully," he said, as the low flame began to heat the murky brew and bubbles appeared along one side of the perimeter.

"There, do you see?" he said, pointing to the bubbles.

"When the edge begins to smile like that—see the smile? When it smiles, lift the tin from the flame for a few seconds," he said, obeying his own instructions.

Though Hafiz was Turkish, the mannerisms of his French schooling abroad hadn't left him—the thin scarf he draped delicately around his neck, his pouted lips, his intense eye contact.

"Are you watching? Keep watching," he said, returning the tin to the flame, where a mystifying alchemy pushed bronze clouds of froth toward the top.

"On the third time, it is finished, but we are not done," Hafiz said, pointing to Baba's special miniature white cup in the open cupboard.

Following his instructions, I placed the cup on the counter and held it steady, while Hafiz poured the coffee at a special angle to ensure that the black sludge, used for fortune-telling by some, made its way to the bottom.

"Now, put it on the tray like this," Hafiz said, setting it on a silver tray with a paper napkin folded into a triangle underneath it. Hafiz lifted the tray and put it in my hands, preparing me to make my grand entrance.

"Here, take this," he said, draping a white cloth napkin over my shoulder.

"Thank you, Hafiz," I said.

"A pleasure—but next time, you're on your own," he said.

When I got to the threshold of the door, despite the weight of the tray, I was still able to bow slightly forward, with my right big toe covering the left toe (a Mevlevi must!), and ask for permission to enter. This gesture is made in remembrance of Rumi's cook who once ran out of stovewood and used his own left toe as fuel to cook for Rumi's dervishes. The cook felt no pain until the moment he doubted the miracle and pulled his burnt toe from the fire—covering it with his right foot when greeting Rumi. After I bowed toward Baba, he bowed his head back at me to accept me into the room.

Miraculously managing to climb over a sea of sitting dervishes and make it to Baba's side without dropping the tray, I knelt on my right knee, kissed the cup, and placed it in front of him.

"Did you watch carefully?" Baba said. I nodded.

"I hope so," he said, "because next time you'll have to make it on your own."

Baba took a sip of the coffee and licked his lips. Though he didn't smile, it seemed to have been brewed to his liking.

"The most important thing," Baba said, "is to make it with love—and a sincere intention."

It was no small feat making Turkish coffee and tea for all of the dervishes and guests that flooded Baba's apartment in the weeks that followed. Forget three cups of tea: most nights we had to make more than thirty cups of tea! And during the days, Baba's house was often just as full, as he entertained any guests who happened to stop by—whether announced or unannounced.

One afternoon, I served Turkish coffee to a father who drove all the way from Ankara to Istanbul to speak with Baba. The man had made the long drive because his daughter wanted to marry her boyfriend, instead of the man he had chosen for her. After I served them both baklava, I retreated to the kitchen, where the lovesick girl's spying sister was nibbling on her fingernails and hanging on their every word.

"How are the deliberations going?" I said, when I heard the men stop talking.

"Thank God, Baba just told my father that my sister should marry for love," she said, as she texted his answer back to her anxious sister in Ankara.

THE HEART

◆

Rumi practiced a "religion of the heart," as he called it. The heart, for Rumi, is our true spiritual center and the sacred realm of our inner reality. In Rumi's poetry, he often directly addresses his own heart, saying "O heart!" and it speaks back to him of the divine essence. As the Qur'an says, "He knows all that is in the heavens and the earth, and he knows what you conceal and reveal. God knows well the secrets of every heart." To the Sufi, the way to draw nearer to the divine is not through the mind but the heart.

> *Sacrifice intellect in love for the friend!*
> *Intellects are from the direction where he is.*

Experiencing the divine cannot be accomplished through logic, reason, or knowledge gleaned from books. On the contrary, the intellect must be abandoned and sacrificed in love for the beloved! That does not mean the intellect is not a vehicle of its own toward knowledge and truth—but it can only go so far. A mystic tries to draw everything toward her heart—her attention, her breath, and her very being.

> *My wandering heart went around the world—*
> *it traveled far seeking my remedy.*
> *But in the end, that sweet and savory water of life*
> *simmered and flowed from the granite of my own heart.*

Through a blessed alchemy, a Sufi's heart transforms from a block of granite to a gushing ocean of love. A dervish worries about not just her own heart but the hearts of others as well—treading with care not to hurt anyone else's heart. Rumi's poetry forces us to ask ourselves if we really have cultivated a warm and loving heart.

> *From these hearts of stone, no heart has yet softened.*
> *From those with the character of ice, none has yet become warm.*
> *Do not tan this leather just yet—*
> *no one yet has any shame from God.*

Dervishes see everything in the universe, including themselves, through the prism of the heart. In reading the Qur'an, they interpret the stories of the prophets through the prism of the heart. In interpreting waking visions and dreams, they read them as signs of the state of the heart. In performing the obligatory rituals and practices of Islam, they stress their effects on expanding and purifying the heart.

> *Every heart in which love for you is not hidden,*
> *is an infidel and not a Muslim.*
> *Any city in which there is not awe of the sultan,*
> *you may assume has been destroyed,*
> *even if it is not in ruins.*

At the level of shari'a, or Islamic law, a heart knows that there is nothing in the world that can be worshipped with certainty except God. The mystic path of Sufism, which dervishes maintain is built upon the foundations of Islamic law, stresses the need for a teacher to guide a mystic to the treasure in her own heart. At this level, the heart begins to understand that there is nothing outside of God. If a mystic advances even further on the path, her heart may reach further levels of revelation, such as divine truth, when the heart seeks after nothing but God and the attainment of mystical knowledge—when the heart rests in the knowledge that nothing exists except God.

> *I've been running out of breath after my heart for so long,*
> *in that place where I had neither existence nor location—*
> *until I lost myself and the world completely.*
> *You could say that with me there is neither this nor that.*

Sufis, like all Muslims, believe that the divine is not contained by heaven or earth but instead can be found in the heart of a faithful, loving servant—a true believer. The divine is not without, but within—closer to a human being than their own jugular vein. As the Qur'an states, "We indeed created man; and we know what his soul whispers within him, and we are nearer to him than the jugular vein." Shams guided Rumi to find the divine within his own heart.

> *The smoke of my heart is the sign of thirsting, O heart!*
> *And this smoke from my heart is unmistakable, O heart!*
> *Every wave that the heart beats of blood, O heart,*
> *is not from a heart but an ocean, O heart!*

A Sufi tries to liberate his heart with every breath from error, worldly preoccupation, and separation from the divine so that the life-giving blood of love can freely flow. Sufis talk about the contraction and expansion of the heart: the heart oscillates between these two phenomena, and each contraction yields an expansion. So if a Sufi is feeling anxious or stuck, and the heart contracts, he can find comfort in knowing that an expansion of the heart will soon follow.

> *Don't be anxious—just feel yourself dreaming,*
> *since thoughts are just veils covering the face of the moon.*
> *The heart is like the moon, so in the heart don't worry!*
> *Toss ruminating into the sea.*

Rumi interrogates his own heart in his poetry to test its devotion to the divine. On the mystic path, the heart must be focused solely on the divine, but Rumi questions whether or not that is true for his own heart. Is his loving devotion sincere and faithful, or does his eye wander?

> *O Lord, what kind of heart is this,*
> *and what character does it have?*
> *What manner of searching and questing*
> *does it have in seeking him?*
> *Every moment this heart bows its head*
> *on the dust of his doorway.*
> *But his dust says: "This heart has a thousand faces!"*

A heart of a thousand faces is not fixed on the divine—but rather looking in all directions in distraction. Such a spiritual seeker is not a faithful and loyal lover. Rumi frequently mentions the lover's desire to be the dust at the door of his beloved. To say you are the dust beneath another is a gesture of humility and devotion: "I am the dust beneath you." The lover longs to be even just the dust beneath the feet of his beloved.

> *I am beautiful—so make yourself beautiful.*
> *Accustom yourself to me and be unaccustomed to others.*

And if you want to be a mine of jewels,
open your heart and make your chest an ocean.

The heart is an ocean filled with pearls and a mine filled
with hidden gems! In a world filled to the brim with worldly
distractions, taking time to remember the divine can feel like
a waste of time, but why would an ailing patient deny himself
such life-giving medicine?

O heart, if you are aware of this story,
what do you expect from this separation of yours?
If you become absent from presence for just one moment,
know that in that moment you are a polytheist on the path.

Every moment that we forget love, we worship a false idol—
the world. We bow down to the forbidden icon of our self. In-
stead of worshipping the one, we worship the many. We choose
the affairs of the world and the desires of our self over the sacred
treasure buried in our own heart—which is love, love, love! The
heart is aware of what it truly needs—love! It knows the healing
that love brings; it craves the sweet nectar of the cure. And yet
still we resist the remedy. Why do we deny our hearts the love
that makes them whole?

I said: O heart, have you fallen into affliction?
It said: I'm well, but what happened to you?
I said: My brain needs a cure.
It said: Oh, you're just crazy because you found the remedy.

For Rumi, rational thought obscures and hides the truth—
it prevents us from living fully from the heart. Rumi de-
scribes the divine beloved as a heart-possessor, a heart-seizer,

and a heart-taker. A dervish offers her heart as a sacrifice to the beloved—she gambles her heart away to win the ultimate treasure.

IF YOU'RE A LOVER

Lovers find certainty staying awake all night until morning,
without food and sleep in pleasant weather.

O friend, if you're a lover, be like a candle—
melt and burn all night long!

Know that he who's like winter weather in autumn
  is anything but a lover—
in the middle of autumn, the lover's heart is in midsummer!

O soul, if you have a love you want to declare—
cry out like a lover! Moan, moan like a lover!

But if you're chained to lust, make no claims to love.
Enter spiritual retreat, and burn off your carnal chains.

O simple-hearted man, how can a lover be attached to lust?
How could Jesus eat from the same muzzle or trough
  as his donkey?

Listen, if you want to detect the fragrance of these riddles—
avert your eyes from everything other than
  Shams al-Din of Tabriz!

But if you can't see that he's greater than the two worlds,
you're still drowned in the ocean of ignorance.

In that case, go study Islamic jurisprudence
with teachers of conventional knowledge
to master the science of:
"This is permitted and that is not."

My soul has traveled far away from childhood
  in love of Shams al-Din—
love for him is not mixed with raisins and nuts.

My intellect has left my writing hand,
  and my verses are now incomplete—
that's why my bow is naked without designs or strings.

O Jalal al-Din, sleep and abandon speech—
no leopard will ever catch that mighty lion!

* * *

Every particle in the air and in the seventh heaven
is for us a rose garden and apple orchard.
While all that's gold is from the shaft of a mine,
every water drop is a talisman with Oman inside.

Despite my lapses and imperfections, Baba said I'd proven my ability to serve, and as a result, he finally invited me to join the whirling practice with the other dervishes—all of whom were men.

"A new period in our lives can start with whirling—with the proper education, whirling can give us energy, patience, and strength," Baba said, placing before me a large, square wooden board with a small knob like a fat, smooth screw in its center.

He sat down to take a sip of his Turkish coffee and looked out the window.

"Whirling, you see, signifies the physical structure of the universe; there is no difference between the universe and its smallest particle, the atom: whatever an atom is, that is the universe," Baba said, wiping the Turkish coffee grinds that got caught in his beard with a white paper napkin.

Baba went on to discuss the motion of electrons, protons, and neutrons. Everything in the whole world, he pointed out, was whirling. He mentioned the revolution of particles, the circulation of blood through the veins, and the return of a soul to its source after death. The difference in the whirling of the dervishes, he said, is that whirling is a *conscious* attempt to be in harmony with all things in nature.

"It is like the sun, moon, stars, galaxies, and world turning around themselves; everything in this universe is whirling—everything revolves," he said. He paused as we marveled at how we are all, at all times, whirling on a giant rock hurling through infinite space around a dying star.

In the mystical whirling ceremony of the Mevlevi Sufi Order, dervishes whirl in a circular formation, much like the planets around the sun, turning counterclockwise. Muslim pilgrims circumambulate counterclockwise around the Kaʿba, the black cube in Mecca, when on hajj—the pilgrimage that Muslims are required to make once in their life in Saudi Arabia if they're financially and physically able. In this sense, dervishes are whirling around the Kaʿba of their own heart. Whirling is very challenging, and it takes patience, endurance, and time to learn.

Following the example of the dervishes whom I had seen go before me, I bowed with my arms hugged across my body with my hands on my shoulders, a gesture that testifies to the oneness of all creation, before kneeling on the polished wooden board and placing a pinch of salt over the knob in the center. Rising to my feet, I bowed one more time before stepping onto the board and placing the knob between the first two toes of my left foot. Due to my freakishly limber joints, I was free from the pain that this knob caused for the other dervishes, who limped in agony up the stairs to Baba's apartment after every practice.

As I slowly dragged my right leg up the calf of my left and placed it down at a perpendicular angle to my left foot, I pivoted 180 degrees. Repeating this action, I returned to my initial starting position, facing the stained-glass windows and Baba. As I looked down at the board, I was surprised to see a perfect circle of salt around the knob, indicating that I'd placed my feet properly. As I continued this very slow meditation in motion, the lids of my eyes fell slightly, veiling the ecstasy I began to feel swelling in my heart.

"Zemzem, what does a dervish look like?" Baba said, encouraging me to step off the board for a break.

Scanning the faces of my dervish brothers for an answer, no answer came. I saw many dervishes standing before me—I knew what they looked like. I was staring right at them—but I knew that wasn't what Baba was asking. An answer eluded me.

"A true dervish has a smiling face, but is full of sorrow; is humble, but dignified; tired, but a fighter; happy, but grieving; sad, but hopeful; quiet, but crying out; with everyone, but alone; alone, but with everyone; poor, but rich; suffering, but helping; wounded, but healing; grounded, yet wandering," he said, picking up the wooden board and putting it back against the wall.

"This is what a dervish looks like," he said, before encouraging me to try whirling again but without the aid of the board. As if it were that easy!

Though I had studied ballet, modern dance, West African

dance, tai chi, and capoeira, trying to whirl without the board felt almost impossible. It required that I integrate my physical, emotional, mental, and spiritual levels of being—taking multi-tasking to a whole new level.

I had to revolve 360 degrees with each step, while inwardly repeating the name of God, and not bump into any other dervishes. In addition, I was being asked, above all, to transcend myself and turn with sincere love and longing toward the beloved.

The other dervishes smiled with encouragement. Humbled, of course, by each sudden stumble, I wobbled like a Weeble in front of Baba and the other dervishes for ten minutes before realizing that I wouldn't be able to juggle these competing tasks through my own will.

The only way to be aware on so many different levels was to surrender to a deeper will that was not my own. Instead of turning, I gradually surrendered to letting myself be turned. Once I felt the gentle push of that invisible hand, there was no stopping me, and I whirled like a spun top for what felt like an eternity.

"Ah, this is what it's like to surrender," I thought, "to let go, and fly."

DON'T SAY ANYTHING

I'm an admirer of the moon—
don't speak about anything but the moon.

In my presence, don't say anything except words
about candles and sugar.

Don't speak words about suffering—
speak no words save those about treasure.

And if you're unaware of this,
don't be distressed—
just don't say anything.

Last night, I became crazy.
Love saw me and said:
"I have come. So don't cry out,
don't tear your garment,
and don't say anything."

I said: " O love! I'm afraid of another thing."
Love replied: "That other thing doesn't exist.
Don't say that other thing.
I will whisper secret words in your ear:
just nod your head 'yes.'
Except for that shake of your head—
don't say anything."

A moon of spiritual attributes
became visible on the path of the heart.

What a gentle journey
there is on the path of the heart.
Don't say anything.

I said: "O heart, what is the moon
*   this heart was pointing to,*
since it is not possible for you to measure?"
"Pass beyond this—
and don't say anything."

I said: "Is this the face of an angel, I wonder,
*   or is it human?"*

My heart said: "This is other than an angel or human.
Don't say anything."

I said: "Tell me: what is this? Or I will fall head over heels!"
My heart said: "Be like this: fall head over heels,
  and don't say anything."

"O you, seated in this house full of images and imagination:
Leap up out of this house, grab your bags, and go.
Don't say anything."

I said, "O heart, be fatherly with me.
Is this not a quality of God?"
My heart said: "It is, but don't say anything
about the soul of a father."

WHIRLING DERVISHES

◆

"Just as food and water are necessary in the time of hunger and thirst, whirling is necessary for the spiritually mature, because it increases their joy for life," Rumi's teacher, Shams, wrote. Shams urged Rumi to put aside religious manuscripts and instead turn to music and ecstatic whirling. Shams himself taught Rumi how to whirl like a dervish. This deep and embodied spiritual practice transformed Rumi from a pious preacher to a passionate lover of God. Consumed with his love of the divine, Rumi, like other whirling dervishes then and now, ascended in his mind, body, and spirit closer to the beloved.

You have become the soul for the soul of this servant.
In the darkness of unbelief, you have become the candle of faith.
In my heart, you have become a singer of melodies.
In my head, you have been dancing like wine.

Rumi uses different words for the movement of whirling in his poetry, but the main word he uses for a session of whirling and poetry accompanied with music—and which is used today to describe the mystical whirling concert of the dervishes of the Mevlevi Sufi Order—is *sema*. The word *sema* means "to listen." In the *sema*, dervishes listen to more than the music being played—they also listen to the song of the divine in their own hearts.

Today is the whirling, the whirling, the whirling!
It is light and radiance, radiance, radiance!
This love is revealed, revealed, revealed!
From the intellect, time to bid farewell, farewell, farewell!

The mystical concert of the whirling dervishes is a meditation in motion—a holistic feast for the hearts of true lovers. It is a blessed reunion between lover and beloved. As Shams explained, "In the people of God, these manifestations and visions are more common during the *Sema*, when they have passed beyond their usual universe of existence. *Sema* carries them out of other universes to the Truth." A whirling dervish strives to see beauty wherever he casts his gaze.

There are many concealed ones in our whirling ceremony—
from the ranks of the Sufis, the wise, and the educated.
But since my wandering heart is both near and far,
no one's running around more than my own unshackled
   heart.

Rumi praised the healing power and spiritual benefits of whirling. Our conditioned thinking, he pointed out, is bound—but not our feet! Movement takes us outside of ourselves and allows us to connect and worship free from the shackles of the mind. As Rumi wrote, "How did you become stuck to the ground like mud? In the end, movement is the key to blessings." In movement, a constricted heart can experience an overpowering expansion. Rumi suggests that love and movement offer us a portal out of the overwhelming sorrows of this world and our own limited minds.

If the whole world were to be filled with sorrow,
that soul who grabs love firmly will be without it.

Look at one particle that has danced in love—
that speck has transformed to conquer the two worlds.

In the microcosm, Rumi perceives the macrocosm: a particle whirling in love contains both the universe and the hereafter. The transformative power of love is without limit.

THE WHIRLING CEREMONY

The whirling ceremony is for the restless soul.
So leap up quickly—
what are you waiting for?

Don't sit here, anxious and distracted.
Go wherever the beloved is—
if you're a real man.

Don't say: "Maybe he doesn't want me."
For what business does a thirsty man have
with such words?

The moth doesn't think about the flame.
For the soul of love, thinking is shameful.

When a man of war hears the call of the drum,
in that moment, he becomes one million times stronger.

You heard the drum, so now draw your spiritual sword!
Your soul is the sheath of the all-conquering Dhu-l-Faqar!

Strike with your sword and take the kingdom of love,
for the kingdom of love is an eternal kingdom.

You are Husayn at Karbala—leave thoughts of water
  behind!
For the "water" today is a burnished sword!

As dervishes whirl in ecstasy, accompanied by singing, chanting, and poetry, they repeat the name of God in their hearts to bring them nearer to the divine—and to help them keep the rhythm required to whirl. Thus, whirling is an inner meditation (with the repetition of "Allah, Allah, Allah") and an outer meditation through movement and sound. It is reported that when the Companions of the Prophet Muhammad asked him, "What are the gardens of Paradise?" the Prophet Muhammad replied, "The circles of meditative remembrance."

The one I'm seeking with tears just for him—
in search of that one, I'm running like a stream.
Today, he came early and said: "Time to whirl."
He didn't even let me make ablution for the morning
  prayer.

As Shams and Rumi liked to practice *sema* together in seclusion (away from the judgmental eyes of jurists, traditionalists, and the envious), it is easy to imagine Shams coming to collect Rumi in the early morning for musical meditation and whirling. Ablution, or ritual washing of the body, is necessary before every morning prayer—but Rumi here suggests that mystic music and whirling supersede the formalistic religious obligation of the morning prayer. This is symbolic and poetic, not literal: Rumi always performed the morning prayer followed by his own personal meditation of reciting: "Allah, Allah, Allah."

The sema has become the gate and way to the heavens.
The sema has been the wings and head for the bird of the soul.
But in your presence, it is really something else—
like performing the prayer behind
the message–bearing Prophet.

For a Sufi, there is no beginning or end to prayer—life itself is a prayer! Every moment and every breath is a prayer! To the mystic, prayer is unending. As Rumi explains, "The prayer time comes five times daily, but the guide for lovers is: be the ones who are continually in prayer!" Rumi practiced and endorsed continuous praying—being in a constant state of bewilderment, gratitude, and praise. Whirling is itself a prayer in motion—an ascension to the divine realm in mind, body, and spirit.

This secret whirling inside our chest—
the wheel of the heavens bows from its rotation.
It knows not the head from the feet or the feet from the head.
It whirls with head and feet and yet without head and feet.

In the sacred whirling dance, dervishes feel logic and language fall away. When you enter the dance, prepare for the veils to fall from your eyes, and the secrets of your true essence—your own unveiled heart—to be revealed.

Sufis often justify this divine dance to more conservative Muslims by referring to a verse in the Qur'an: "To God belong the East and the West, and wherever you turn is the face of God—He is the All-Embracing, the All-Knowing." Rumi even puts *sema* on par with the religious obligations that form the foundation of Islam. Shams similarly wrote that *sema* was a religious necessity, like the fasting of Ramadan and daily prayers, for those who have attained a holy state of mind—a high spiritual rank. Not all mystics were given automatic permission to whirl: only those who were seen to be spiritually mature and not ruled by their ego were granted permission.

> *O you, the soul of the* sema, *the fast, the pilgrimage,*
> *and prayer—*
> *from you, play and metaphor have become truth!*
> *Today I am your musician, O candle of Taraz—*
> *coins are scattering from the wheels of heaven*
>   *for this poor street performer.*

Taraz, a city in Central Asia in modern-day Kazakhstan, was said to be filled in Rumi's day with beautiful people, so "candle of Taraz" was an epithet for the beloved. For Rumi, Shams was the soul of the *sema*—the sun he whirled around.

Sema makes the invisible realm of the heart visible and embodied. This joyful communion of dervish hearts with the divine is a collective spiritual journey that also aims to transport the spirits of all those in attendance to the invisible realm through the sublime beauty of music and dance.

BREAK OUR HARPS

> *Break our harps, O exalted ones!*
> *Thousands of other harps are here!*
>
> *When we're gripped by the clutches of love,*
> *how could we ever be short of harps and flutes?*
>
> *Even if all the rebabs and harps of the world burned up,*
> *there are so many hidden harps in the heart, my friend!*
>
> *Their strumming goes up to the heavens,*
> *though their music doesn't enter the ears of the deaf.*

Even if all the lamps and candles of the world
*   were extinguished,*
what sorrow would there be—
since flint and steel are fixed firmly in existence?

Songs are just straw on the face of sea—
no pearl floats to the surface of the ocean.

But know that the grace of the straw
comes from the pearl—
upon us is the reflection of the reflection of his gleam.

All songs are just branches of the yearning for union—
but branch and root are never equal.

Close your mouth and open the window of your heart—
and in that way,
converse with the spirits.

Whirling is a plea with the whole body for union with the divine. In whirling around the heart and one another like spinning planets, a shaykh and his dervishes send blessings to all travelers on the way of love from their revolving hearts. *Sema* is a communal practice: while soaring spiritually to the heavens, a whirling dervish must be aware of the others whirling around her and those in attendance. As Shams wrote, "If one of the mature ones begins to whirl in the East, another one starts moving in the West. They are aware of each other's state."

The moment I'm whirling around you—
*   is a communion of cupbearer, wine, cup,*
*   and the whirling of wine.*

And the instant the brilliance of your benevolence is revealed—
my soul becomes bewildered like Moses of Imran.

Moses is mentioned in the Qur'an more than any other
prophet, and for dervishes he is an exemplary spiritual wayfarer
and mystic interpreter of divine signs. When witnessing God
miraculously turn a mountain to ash, Moses experiences such
a state of bewilderment that he loses consciousness. That is the
mystical state from which Sufis draw inspiration. In whirling, a
dervish tries to become bewildered, enraptured, and obliterated
by the overwhelming glory, power, and beauty of divine love.

HOW DO YOU KNOW?

How do you know which birds we are,
or what we sing every moment under our breath?

How can anyone bring us to hand?
Sometimes we are the treasure,
other times, destroyed.

The heavens rotate for our sake.
For this reason, we keep turning like a wheel.

How should we remain in this house—
when in this house we are all guests?

Although in form we are beggars in the lane of love,
behold the attributes that make us sultan.

Why should we have sorrow
that we are imprisoned today,
when tomorrow we will be king of all Egypt?

As long as we've been in this form,
no one has troubled us,
and we haven't troubled anyone else.

When Shams of Tabriz becomes our guest,
we are hundreds of millions of times untroubled and free.

Love, of course, is not linear; it is a dance with no script, choreography, or clear beginning or end. A dervish heart whirls in circles, flitting with yearning like a moth around a flame, as it draws nearer to the object of its affection. Love is an improvisation between hearts listening with care to the beauty and magic arising between them. In Rumi's mind, the mystic heart is completely dependent upon the beloved—with his every move dictated by his beloved.

I don't know how to drink wine without your face.
I don't know how to take a chess piece without your hand.
Far from me, you keep commanding me to dance.
But without your melody, I don't know how to dance.

In addition to Rumi's many verses celebrating whirling, Rumi's poems also extol the ecstatic power and intoxicating beauty of music. In fact, he drew inspiration from musical rhythms to shape the meters of his poetry. Rumi himself was a talented musician, and he loved to play the rebab. To Rumi, the rebab is the creaking sound of the door of paradise opening!

Since I have known the fire and water of love,
into the fire of the heart I have dissolved like water.
Like a rebab, I have emptied my whole heart.
I am custom-made to the pluck of love's wound.

Though the rebab is empty, it makes beautiful music; this image is Rumi's inspiration for a dervish heart—empty of self but receptive to being of service and producing beauty in the hands of the divine. In a story in *The Masnavi* about a poor man who began to pray when he became empty, Rumi writes: "The Prophet has said that the true believer is a lute that makes music at the time it is empty." Rumi also paints music as a remedy for rumination and the secret to peace of mind, as it uplifts the soul.

> *Today, like every day, we are wasted—ruined!*
> *Don't open the door of rumination—take up the rebab instead.*
> *There are a hundred kinds of prayer, bowing, and prostration*
> *for the one whose prayer niche is the beauty of the beloved.*

In fact, Rumi's son Sultan Walad began one of his own works with the verse, "Listen to the various points of love from the rebab's weeping and groaning." For Rumi and his son, the rebab and the reed flute both moan and cry out as if yearning to be reunited with the beloved!

During Rumi's time, there were suggested rules of conduct for *sema*. Good fragrances were encouraged; even today many Sufi lodges and graves of Sufi masters are bathed in rose essence. As for the audience at a *sema*, all those who loved mystics were welcome to attend. This did not just include the mystically initiated, as many who were drawn to the beauty of Sufism did not have the perceived maturity, strength, or capacity to adopt Sufi discipline and practices. It should be noted, however, that in Rumi's time beardless male youths and women were often discouraged from attending *sema*, as they were seen as objects of temptation. Rumi, however, attended female whirling gatherings in Konya.

Dervish manuals laid out the proper etiquette for those in

attendance listening to and watching the whirling: they should be attentive, still, and silent, and should bow their heads in contemplation and appreciation of the blessings of love's beauty and bounty. However, Rumi also mentions hand-clapping by those in attendance—as well as shouts of ecstasy by dervishes whirling.

> *God forbid the heart of the lover should ever be sorrowful,*
> *or his robe torn—except by love.*
> *God forbid a lover should ever sleep in the dust.*
> *Since he is pure, where will he go?*
> *To the world of purity.*

One practice during Rumi's day that does not happen today in most *sema* ceremonies was the controversial custom of tearing off one's pockets or clothing or even the shirt or hem of another's robe while in a state of ecstasy. This pre-Islamic practice was used to express extreme emotions, and it did find its way into *sema*. In medieval Sufism, this spontaneous act was referred to as the "tearing of the garments" or "uncovering the chest." Such unorthodox behavior obviously attracted criticism and scorn from Muslims who did not approve of such practices. In his poems, Rumi turns this act into a poetic symbol of a dervish heart becoming completely consumed with love of the divine.

> *Strike the bow of your heart!*
> *May your heart tremble with love*
> *like a tambourine.*
> *Let yourself be held like a harp*
> *in the lap of love.*

Music and dance were seen by many medieval Muslim theologians as heretical innovations and vehicles of Satan—a view that certain sects and communities of Muslims still hold today. Rumi had broken from his father's more traditional stance by practicing *sema* in both Damascus and Konya. It was during Rumi's time in Damascus that he began to transform into a mystic—going beyond the letter of the law to the spirit of the law in his reorientation from the particulars of jurisprudence to complete absorption in love. While Rumi's father was accepting of Sufis and had a heart oriented toward mysticism, he did not favor allowing music and dance as a form of worship.

> *I was an ascetic, until you made me a singer.*
> *You made me the life of the party, and a lover of wine.*
> *I used to sit with dignity on the prayer rug.*
> *Then you made me a toy for children of the neighborhood.*

Rumi's teacher, Shams, was also a staunch defender of *sema*. He wrote, "It is blasphemy to say that the *Sema* performed by God's people is a sin. That hand which moves without the Divine exuberance will burn in hell for sure, and the hands that rise in *Sema* will reach paradise—for sure."[4] Defenses of *sema* in medieval dervish manuals included the fact that beautiful sounds are allowed in Islam, poetry recitation is allowed according to the Sayings of the Prophet, and appreciation of the blessings of beauty is incumbent upon a believer. Shams even warned about criticizing or forbidding the *sema*:

> The shaykh said, "The Caliph has forbidden the *Sema*." This prohibition turned into a knot within a certain dervish. He fell ill and they took him to a specialist. He examined his pulse and looked for the cause of illness. It was like nothing he had ever learned about. He couldn't find anything wrong with him, but the dervish died. Afterward, the doctor

performed an autopsy and found the knot within his chest. It had become a carnelian. The doctor kept this gem until a time when he needed some extra cash. The gem passed from hand to hand until it reached the caliph, who had the gem set into a ring. One day, that same caliph was attending a *Sema*, watching from above, when he discovered that his clothes were covered with blood. He examined himself but could find no wound anywhere. He felt for his ring and the stone was gone. Later they traced that gem back to its original owner and the doctor told them the whole story mentioned above.[5]

After Shams disappeared forever one night under mysterious circumstances, Rumi tried to feel close to him by practicing *sema* as they had done together in seclusion behind closed doors. Did Rumi's followers murder Shams? Did his jealous son, 'Ala al-Din? Did Shams pack up and leave? Rumi never found out the truth of what happened. In his sorrow, Rumi whirled and meditated day and night, sacrificing sleep to cry out constantly for his missing spiritual master. Whirling was solace for his sorrow and comfort for his grief. He never again saw his beloved Shams.

As Rumi whirled and whirled in grief over his separation from his beloved Shams, his heart began to compose the most celebrated verses in the Persian language. As Rumi knew well, whirling is a healing modality—a holistic treatment for the mind, body, and soul. In fact, the celebrated medieval Muslim philosopher Abu Hamid al-Ghazali, whose legacy and writing Rumi was exposed to in Baghdad, turned to whirling himself when he left his prestigious teaching post and journeyed to Damascus and Jerusalem to immerse himself completely in mysticism, meditation, and spiritual exercises. It was whirling that helped him heal from his own despair and revive his spiritual life.

While a typical Muslim funeral traditionally features a solemn recitation of the Qur'an and a declaration that the deceased was a believer who died a Muslim, Rumi asked for singing and whirling at his own funeral procession—which the more "orthodox" Muslim community of Konya found appalling. Rumi had requested that his funeral procession bring kettledrums, flutes, and tambourines to usher his body to his grave with whirling and sacred songs. The friends of God, he wanted to show, dance toward eternity in the joy of spiritual communion—ready to meet the beloved as not just "Muslims" but also "lovers."

THE WHIRLING MOOD

I saw the noble face of the beloved,
which is like a garden full of flowers—
an eye for me to see,
and a lamp to enlighten me.

The one who is the qibla,
the prayer direction toward which
my soul prostrates.

My heart told me to abandon life right there—
to leave behind existence and "I"-ness.

In ecstasy, my soul entered the mood of the sema,
and started to clap.

Then love arrived and said:
"What can I do in this
lovely and joyous setting?"

The institutionalization of the Mevlevi Sufi Order began under Rumi's son Sultan Walad (Shaykh Baha al-Din Walad) and crystallized in the sixteenth century. Sultan Walad had also been a disciple of Shams of Tabriz, who once said, "I gave my head to Mawlana [Rumi] and my secret to Sultan Walad." Sultan Walad was less of an "ecstatic" Sufi than his father, Rumi, was, but his interest in and attention to organization, formality, and ritual helped to give a strong foundation to the order founded in Rumi's memory.

Rumi's son standardized the Sufi practices of the order and systematized his teachings. In his writings, Sultan Walad wrote about the development of the Mevlevi Sufi Order, the fundamentals of mysticism, the proper rules of dervish conduct, and Islamic law. Sultan Walad transformed Rumi's mystical, freewheeling spiritual artistic movement into a powerful institution that stretched across the region.

Sultan Walad was also a poet, and he wrote in Persian, Arabic, Turkish, and Greek. Sultan Walad lived in a golden age of Sufism, during the best years of the Seljuks' rule, in which many of the founders of great Sufi orders lived. Like his father, Sultan Walad had female mystic disciples.

While the Mevlevis became a well-established Sufi order in the Ottoman Empire, the practice of legalized whirling ended with the overthrow of the Ottoman Empire, when Kemal Ataturk declared all forms of communal Sufi devotion illegal—to prevent these highly structured spiritual communities and their leaders from posing a challenge to the centrality and power of the state. The Amendment of 1925, created by President Kemal Ataturk, banned all Sufi orders to limit their political power and influence. At the time, popular Sufi masters had thousands of disciples, and this posed a threat to the authority of the state. In the eyes of Turkey's secular leader, Sufis were the antithesis of modernity—relics of an Ottoman past that needed to be discarded for the country to progress.

Even though Sufism was criminalized and the Sufi endowments were confiscated, Rumi's shrine complex in Konya where he is buried was allowed to reopen in 1927. It still holds the official status of a "museum." The *sema* ceremony was allowed to be performed again in public in the 1950s as a "cultural" and "musical" performance. Sufism is currently still illegal in Turkey, based on the law that Ataturk passed in 1925 putting an end to meeting and whirling in dervish lodges, caring after the tombs of holy people, visiting shaykhs, and initiating Sufis into Sufi orders. "I would be fired if my colleagues ever found out that I come here and practice Sufism," a university professor sitting next to me at a *sema* once whispered to me in confidence as the dervishes took flight.

ENTER AMONG US

Enter among us, for we are the lovers,
so we may draw open the gate
of the garden of love for you.

Become a resident in our home, like a shadow,
so we may be neighbors of the sun.

Like the soul in the world,
we are invisible.
Though we are signless,
like the love of lovers,
our traces are always with you—
since we are both hidden and manifest,
like the soul.

Anything you say about us,
such as: "You are that,"
look higher,
for we are higher than that.

You are a waterway—
but a whirlpool and
imprisoned.
Enter among us,
for we are a flowing flood.

Since we've lost everything
in our spiritual poverty,
we're unable to do anything
except compose poems
about not-knowing.

* * *

The whirling has become the food of the lovers,
for in it is the image of reunion.

Every day in my retreat, Baba had me practicing whirling in his presence and alone. When my whirling outfit finally arrived in the hands of a nimble tailor who was responsible for sewing all the gowns for Baba's whirling dervish disciples, Baba took it ceremoniously in his hand with great care. He kissed the base of the camel-hair hat, shaped like a tombstone to represent the death of the ego, and told me to kneel before him.

"Sufism is the rose garden of love. Whoever seeks with a pure heart will find what they are looking for; the goal is to find the light behind the sun," he said, kissing it again, and placing it on my head.

To try on the rest of the outfit in private, I hurried to my room to drape my body in the wide, white dress that symbolizes the death shroud of the ego. Some of my dervish brothers waited outside my door, and then came in when I was dressed to help me make adjustments and tie the white cummerbund around my waist. Staring at myself in the mirror, dressed in those symbolic funeral garments, I couldn't help but smile.

It appeared that my obsession with death was serving me well on the Sufi path. I hadn't had to relinquish it—just redirect it. My dervish brothers grabbed the hem of my white skirt to save it from the dusty stairs, as we scampered upstairs to show Baba.

As I entered, Baba and the other dervishes bowed in my direction, oohing and aahing in Turkish and giving me a dozen thumbs-up. Though the robes don't make a dervish, for the first time I no longer felt like a Sufi impostor or intruder. I finally belonged, inside and out.

"Welcome, *semazen* Zemzem," Baba said, finally bestowing upon me the title *semazen*—one who has been given permission to perform *sema*, the whirling ceremony.

Under Baba's patient guidance, I had been transformed into one who listens, one who surrenders, and one who whirls and dances in both brokenness and wholeness, suffering and wellness, life and death.

My Sufi fashion show lasted only so long. Baba called for us to follow him to the basement to perform a whirling ceremony. But first, Baba said that I would have to undergo a traditional whirling test to be accepted as a true *semazen*. My dervish brothers, dressed in their own ceremonial white garb, lined up and looked on supportively, as Baba asked me to whirl 1,001 times in the center of the room without stopping.

I stepped to the center of the room and bowed in front of Baba. He bowed in return. Taking a deep breath, before launching into a thousand turns, I began to whirl several times with my arms crossed over my chest before unfolding them to take flight. As beads of sweat cascaded down my back from the heat of whirling in a weighted skirt—no one had warned me how heavy it would be—I closed my eyes and timed my breathing to my steps.

Baba, the dervishes, and every object in the room soon disappeared as my eyes relinquished their focus to behold the breeze of flashing colors whirling around me. Was I whirling, or was the room? Who was counting, and did it even matter? I felt like I could whirl for eternity—and if no one stopped me, maybe I would.

But after 500 turns, I began to slightly lose my balance and doubted I had the stamina to continue. I could feel the support of my dervish brothers rooting me on, though I couldn't make out their faces or forms. One step, I thought. Just one step. I tried focusing on just one step at a time. All that was required, I realized, was one step. Being fully present—not worrying about passing a test, or even "whirling." Just one step. One step, and I could take flight.

Before I knew it, I was once again being turned, instead of turning. When I finally finished 1,001 rotations, I managed to stop on a dime and bow in Baba's direction, before stumbling over dizzily, as if drunk, to join the other dervishes in line. After a month of training, I'd finally done it—I'd become a true *semazen*—in mind, body, and spirit.

After my dervish brothers heartily congratulated me, we took our places for the whirling ceremony. While spiritual whirling traditions existed in Central Asia before Islam emerged, the whirling of the Mevlevi Sufi Order today is a highly structured ceremony of prayer. In this ritual encoded with symbolism, every aspect of the movements and clothing is endowed with meaning. Entering the space with our arms crossed in front of our bodies, to represent the number one, we testified in our minds, bodies, and souls to the unity of all existence.

After we took our places on the sheepskins on the ground, one of the senior dervishes sang a eulogy to the Prophet, who Sufis consider the ultimate representative of love. This serene and soulful eulogy was followed by a formidable beat on the small drums, symbolizing the divine command to "Be!" The *ney*, or reed flute, sang its sorrowful tale of being plucked and separated from its source, the reed-bed, to remind us that we too had been sent forth from the source of love, to whom we all longed to return.

Rising, we walked three times in a circle around the space, slowly bowing to each other each time we passed by Baba, who stood like a guard in front of his red sheepskin post. In this salutation of soul to soul, we acknowledged the divine essence in each heart present in the circle. After these three rotations, we removed our black cloaks, symbolizing the world of materiality and darkness, to be reborn to the truth in our pure white whirling gowns. The only way to take flight was to leave the world behind.

One by one, we stretched our arms to the sky, with our right palms open to receive God's love and compassion, and our left ones turned downward to transmit God's love from above to the earth. Revolving around our hearts, counterclockwise like the planets around the sun, we traveled in unison toward the spiritual sun of the worlds.

While we whirled in unison, Baba stepped forward and internally recited a prayer for all travelers on the way of love.

Baba gradually joined in our cosmic dance by walking slowly into the center to take his place as the representative of the sun. Whirling ever so slowly, Baba opened the left side of his cloak to radiate light and love from his heart to all those in attendance and the world.

When our whirling came to a close, our arms returned to the position where they first began: consciously and humbly crossed in front of our chests—testifying to the unity of all existence. After our final bow in Baba's direction, Hafiz recited a verse from the Qur'an: "To God belong the East and the West, and wherever you turn is the face of God—He is the All-Embracing, the All-Knowing." Baba ended the ceremony with a prayer for peace as we sank into the stillness, wrapped up again in our dark robes—having returned from the heights of ecstasy to bring the light and love of the heavens back with us to earth.

SEARCH FOR THAT ONE

The eye must search for that one
to see an amazing thing.

And the soul must search for that one
to experience pleasure and joy.

The head must search for that one
to become drunk for an idol.
Or it must search for that one
to experience pain
for the sake of the friend.

Love must search for that one
to fly to the heavens.

And the intellect must search for that one
to find knowledge and manners.

The secrets and wonders are beyond causes,
and the eye is veiled,
for all it can see is causes.

The lover on this way who becomes disreputable
with a hundred accusations upon him—
when the time for union comes,
will find a hundred names and nicknames.

It's worth wandering through the desert sands for hajj.
One adapts to the milk of camels,
and plundering of Arabs.

The pilgrim places a kiss from her heart on the Black Stone,
to experience the pleasure of her lips
    on the ruby lips of the friend.

As for the coin of the beloved's speech,
take care and don't mint any other—
for only the one who can see the gold mine
has the desire for it.

LOVE

———————◆———————

Rumi's poems have been misunderstood in the West as romantic love poems, in part because sexual language was added to them and religious references were stripped from them in popular translations. However, Rumi wrote his mystical poetry as an expression of his insatiable love for the divine and all creation. His inspiration and model for this love was his teacher, Shams of Tabriz. In his heartfelt verses of love and longing, Rumi invites us to turn away from worshipping the world and the body and instead become devoted servants in the everlasting kingdom of love.

Hey you, who is alive by the soul of this world.
Shame on you! Why do you live this way?
Don't live without love, and you won't become a corpse.
Die in love and alive you shall remain!

On the mystic path, love is an attribute of the divine. Human love is merely a reflection of divine love. As God says in the Islamic tradition, "I was a hidden treasure, and I wished to be known, so I created creation, then made myself known to them, and they recognized me." It is the human heart—not the rational mind—that perceives and recognizes the loving essence of the divine transcendent reality.

AMONG THE LOVERS

Among lovers, don't be rational—
especially when in love with such a sweet face!

Let the rational people stay far from the lovers.
May the soiled earth be far from the gentle breeze!

If a rational person enters,
tell him there is no way.

But if a lover comes in,
give him a hundred welcomes!

By the time a rational person has strategized
   and deliberated,
love has already flown to the seventh heaven.

And by the time a reasonable person has found
   a camel for hajj,
love has already climbed Mount Safa.

Love has come and closed my mouth.
Pass beyond poetry and fly to the stars!

For Rumi, love is the way—it is the path and the purpose.
Love, love, love! Love is all—and all is love! Rumi asks us to
consider: What is the point of life—if it is not lived with love?
Without love, we are nothing but the walking dead.

Love is an attribute of God who is without need.
Love for anything but him is metaphorical.

In Abu Hamid al-Ghazali's *The Revival of the Religious Sciences,* al-Ghazali writes about love, longing, intimacy, and contentment, and he makes the case that all spiritual stages and virtues such as patience, gratitude, and repentance lead, ultimately, to love. Rumi, whose father admired al-Ghazali's writing and mystic philosophy, was influenced by his insistence on the necessity of loving God as the ultimate goal.

> *The way of love is a secret: there's no legal dispute*
>   *about it,*
> *because there's no description of it—just spiritual meaning.*
> *For the lover, there's no answer from religious decrees.*
> *Because this issue is about nonexistence—not existence.*

Fatwas, which are Islamic legal opinions, cannot provide answers or guidance to the one whose heart is immersed in the divine reality of boundless love. The only way to unlock the secret of love is to experience it for yourself. As Shams explained, "Something reaches you" from "the Eternal One." What is it that reaches us? "Well, it is love. The trap of love comes and embraces you," he explained.

YOU'VE BECOME A LOVER

You've become a lover, O heart!
May your passion be blessed!

You've transcended place and location.
May that place of yours be blessed!

Pass beyond both this world and the
  next.

Eat and play alone so the heavenly kingdom
and angels may say:
"May your solitude be blessed!"

O foremost chief of manhood,
today you've eaten the fruit.
O abstainer from tomorrowness,
may your future be blessed!

Your unbelief completely became
    religion.
Your bitterness became entirely
    sweetness.
You've become wholly halva.
May your halva be blessed!

In the dervish lodge of the heart,
the dervishes are in ecstatic uproar!

O heart without hatred,
may your ecstatic cries be blessed!

This heart-seeing eye was a teardrop,
but became an ocean.
Its ocean is saying:
"May your ocean be blessed!"

O hidden lover,
may that friend become your companion!
O seeker of transcendence,
may your transcendence be blessed!

O admired soul, seeking and striving:
your wings have grown.
May your wings be blessed!

Now, be silent and hidden.
You've done well in the bazaar,
and carried off many amazing goods.
May your merchandise be blessed!

A Sufi's lament for greater intimacy with the beloved is endless: pages cannot contain it. Just as a dervish's heart turns to the divine in love, so too does God love to be known and remembered. As the Qur'an states, "They love God, and God loves them."

All the paper of Egypt and Baghdad, O dear one,
I've filled with my pleas and laments, O dear one.
An hour of love is worth more than a hundred worlds.
May a hundred lives be sacrificed for love, O dear one!

Free from the burdens and demands of the world and self, a dervish dives completely into the ocean of love with no longing for the shore. What shore? There is no shore—only love! In the embrace of the beloved, the dervish floats in the eternal realm of love.

Love is the way and the path of our Prophet.
Of love we were born and love became our mother.
O our mother, hidden in veils—
concealed from our unbelieving natures.

For Rumi, the path of the Prophet Muhammad is love. Islam is love. The mystic way is love. The beloved is love. Our origin is love. Our essence is love. All is love! Love is perfect by

its very nature: it is complete. It is real. It is truth. It is our self
that is not complete or real—because the self is an illusion.

This love is complete, complete, complete!
And this self is imaginary, imaginary, imaginary!
This light is majestic, majestic, majestic!
And today there is union, union, union!

The ego is the obstacle to being completely felled by all-
consuming love. The ego blocks the majestic light of truth. It
keeps us separate from our source and one another. The ego is
imaginary—but love, light, and union are eternal and real.

In love, first the part sings a song—then the whole.
In the garden, the unripe grape is first—then the wine.
O heart, this is the rule in springtime.
The cat becomes frisky and then the nightingale.

Rumi captures how our base lust can be transformed into
a more refined love of the eternal beloved, through his poetic
images of the frisky cat in heat and the nightingale. Our soul
begins the spiritual path heavy with uncontrollable desire for
the temptations of the world but then it transforms and flies to
higher realms. We begin unripe and unready—but through a
blessed alchemy, we are transformed into sweet wine.

But to transform, we must first take a courageous step to-
ward love. Rumi asks us to consider: Why gaze at love from
afar? For how long will you contemplate the ocean before diving
in? Why deny yourself the greatest medicine of all?

For how long will you be my onlooker from afar?
I am the generous remedy and love is my incurable one.

What is the soul? The smallest child in my cradle.
What is the heart? One of my foreign outcasts.

The lover is in exile from the world, wandering in search of the beloved—with no concern for borders or the dictates of society. A dervish heart chooses self-exile from the temptations, conventions, and comforts of the world to take refuge in the sanctuary of love.

O love, souls are from traces of your spirit.
O love, salts are from your salt shaker.
O love, all gold pieces are from your mine.
You are the clothed one and the whole crowd is naked.

For the mystic, everything originates from the source of love. Meander through the meetings of Muslim mystics, in any corner of the world, and you'll find them intoxicated on love. In their circles of meditation and divine remembrance, they become drunk with the ecstasy of love—and cry out with longing for their beloved.

Wander through the inns and peer into the taverns.
Observe the hugs of the drunkards in meetings.
In the Ka'ba of love, look toward the confirmed place—
hear the cries from the spirit and drink in the shouting.

As the black cube at Mecca that Muslims on pilgrimage circumambulate, the Ka'ba is, in a sense, the heart of Islamic practice on the physical plane. But for Rumi, the mystic gathering of dervishes is the Ka'ba of love—where yearning hearts commune and cry out in love.

God forbid the heart of love ever looks upon the world!
What is there to look upon except love?
I will reject my eyes on the day of death,
if they abandon love in gazing at life.

A mystic heart perceives only love. Rumi asks us to consider: Why focus our eyes for even a moment on the material world—with its temptations, brokenness, and strife? Before death comes, Rumi says, make love the sole object of your attention and gaze!

If I give my life for your sake, I'll die well.
And if I'm the slave of your slave, I'll be a happy prince.
I'm crazy from those two curls like chains.
I'm entranced by those two eyes,
enchanted by magicians from Kashmir.

Kashmir was seen in Rumi's time as a place of magic. It was an imagined landscape of enchantment and seduction. Entranced by the mystical charms of the beloved, a lover realizes that he must let his self die to draw nearer in passionate submission to the master of his heart.

There is a difference, for the mystic, in faith in the divine and love of the divine. When a heart operates from love, it is dynamic and awakened in its relationship with the divine. It does not merely follow doctrine or affirm a set of beliefs—instead, it is passionately consumed with its connection to the divine.

I have love of you instead of faith.
As long as I have life, my soul can't abstain from love.
I said: I promise not to bother you for two or three days.

But I was unable to resist.
What can I keep hidden from you?

To the mystic, love eclipses everything else—because everything is love. While Rumi paints the relationship between the lover and beloved as intimate, this does not mean that the lover and beloved are on equal footing. Unlike human beings, the divine essence is not in need. As Shams explained:

What is it worth to bring cumin to the city of Kerman? Who will it make happy? What will it cost? There is such a great palace there, one without prayers or wishes. He does not expect anything from anybody. But you bring prayers to Him, because that Court that is without any need likes your prayers and wishes.

Just as the Persian city of Kerman has vast quantities of cumin and is in need of no more, so too is the divine presence without need for acquisition—or anything, for that matter. The beloved exists without need or expectation, but appreciates and is pleased by loving acts of devotion and remembrance in the hearts of his lovers.

Your love could slay Turks and Arabs.
I'm the admirer of those martyrs and warriors.
Your love said: "No one can win his soul from me."
Truly it said: "O heart, abandon this game!"

Rumi writes about mystics as martyrs and warriors who have died on the battlefield of love. We must give our souls to love, Rumi suggests, and abandon our impulse for separateness in favor of union. In every moment, we must give ourselves away to love.

We found our healing balm in love—
and now sacrifice our breaths every second to love,
so every breath of ours may go toward love.
Love finds its own breath in our every breath.

For mystics, there is no better cure than love. Every breath is offered—and sacrificed—to love. Who is the one breathing? For the mystic who has annihilated the self, love itself becomes the breath. Love itself is the inhale and love itself is the exhale.

We've read many fairy tales and nighttime stories
about lovers, beloveds, and the sorrow of the wounded heart.
But the foundation of the flag of love is all love for you.
You are different, king, and love for you is different.

We all grow up with fairy tales of love—but, for Rumi, the greatest love story of all is the love between the human heart and the divine. All loves flow from that love. Rumi grew up with stories that featured legendary kings and warriors, as well as demons, genies, and angels. He was well versed in the stories of the day, from star-crossed lovers to animal fables. But, as Rumi notes, the story of the heart and soul cannot be told with mere words.

Tonight, remove the veils at once!
Tonight, don't let a strand of hair of this world
    or the next remain!
Yesterday, you told the story of the heart and soul.
Tonight, we will lay them before you—
killed and lamentable.

True lovers have no need to hide any aspect of themselves—they are open books, because they are no longer attached to the

whims of the ego, the pride of reputation, or the comfort of con-
cealment. Throw off the veils, Rumi says, and kill your stories
and ideas about love—and instead: become love itself.

> *The one who is aware of the secret of loverhood,*
> *is well-known and famous among the lovers.*
> *But the one who hides himself to protect his reputation*
> *will clearly be every which way in separation.*

To those who dare to be vulnerable, the secret of loverhood
is unveiled to their hearts, and they are warmly welcomed into
the embrace of the luminous circle of lovers. Those, however, who
fixate on managing their reputations and egos suffer in separation.

> *Where is the mind of the lover? Toward the breeze.*
> *Where is the mind of the rational one? With silver and gold.*
> *Where is the place of flowers? The garden and paradise.*
> *Where is the place of firewood? The depths of hell.*

The true treasure for the dervish is not money and success but
rather blissful emanations of the beloved from the unseen realm.
A mind driven by reason searches for profit and gain—but a
mind steered by love retreats from the material world to seek the
sweet breeze of the beloved and is caressed by its gentle beauty.

> *In love, there's neither high nor low—*
> *consciousness nor unconsciousness.*
> *There's no reciter of the Qur'an, shaykh, or disciple—*
> *just hooliganism, roguery, and belittling oneself.*

On the path of love, there is nothing but oneness—no hierar-
chy, no division, no identity. Sleeping and waking, consciousness

and unconsciousness, master and disciple—all duality collapses
in the face of the one. A true lover wears the mantle of humility
and brings herself down low; she knows that the ultimate wis-
dom is to be found in the mocking of one's self and even being a
buffoon. Free from all pretense and anxiety over reputation, she
relishes being a rogue.

O LOVERS!

O lovers! O lovers!
I turn dust into gems.
O musicians! O musicians!
I'll fill your tambourines with gold.

O thirsty souls! O thirsty souls!
Today I'm the wine pourer,
and this spiritless dustbin
I'll transform into heaven—
a river in paradise.

O lonely ones! O lonely ones!
Relief has come! Relief has come!
I turn everyone who's wounded
and distressed into a sultan—a Sanjar!

O alchemy! O alchemy!
Look at me, for I turn a hundred
monasteries into mosques,
a hundred gallows into pulpits!

O unbelievers! O unbelievers!
Unfasten your locks!

For I am the absolute ruler:
I make some believers,
and others infidels!

O pal! O pal!
You're wax in my hands!
If you become a dagger,
I'll make you into a goblet.
And if you become a goblet,
I'll make you into a dagger.

You were sperm and became blood,
then you became a harmonious body.
Come to me, O child of Adam!
I'll make you even more ornate.

I turn grief into happiness,
and guide lost souls.
I turn the wolf into Joseph,
and poison into sugar!

O chief of the drinkers! O chief of the drinkers!
I've opened my mouth to pair every dry lip
with the lips of the wineglass.

O rose garden! O rose garden!
Receive roses from the rose garden—
the moment I marry basil and the lotus.

O heaven! O heaven!
You'll become even more astonished

than the narcissus,
when I turn dust into ambergris—
thorns into jasmine.

O Universal Intellect! O Universal Intellect!
Whatever you say is true.
You are the ruler!
You are the judge!
And then it said to me:
I would speak less.

* * *

The music of the reed flute is from his breath.
The spirit's ecstatic shouts are from his euphoric cries.
If the reed flute hadn't exchanged pillow talk with his lips,
it never would have filled the world with sugar.

"For your dervish education, I want you to start learning how to play the *ney*," Baba said one day, surprising me with a new spiritual musical practice to integrate into my retreat.

As a concert Javanese gamelan player, I had no illusions about how difficult the *ney*, or reed flute, would be to study. While my dervish brothers had spent weeks teaching me how to play the *kudüm*, or small kettledrums, I'd intentionally stayed away from the *ney*—as it's notoriously difficult to learn.

Baba had arranged a lesson for me with a sweet and shy dervish named Kemal, who was waiting for me on Baba's antique love seat and eager to teach me.

Kemal, whose thick auburn hair was twisted in curls that

blended in with the Ottoman calligraphy hanging behind him, placed a delicate *ney* in my hands as I sat down beside him.

"On average, it takes three months for a student to make one sound—and even when a sound emerges, the student must search for their own voice," Kemal said.

"*Lazim sabr,*" Baba said from his kilim cushions on the floor—"patience is necessary."

"Before we start, do you know the opening lines of Rumi's masterpiece, *The Masnavi,* which begins with the voice of the *ney,* lamenting of its separation from its source and its desire to be reunited?" Kemal said, opening up Rumi's masterpiece to those famous lines.

LISTEN TO THE *NEY*

Listen to the ney,
how it sings its story
and laments over separation.

Ever since I was cut from the reedbed,
men and women have been breathing
their cries of sorrows into my songs.

I want a heart ripped to shreds from separation,
so I may relate the pain of yearning desire.

Whoever's been left far from their origin,
seeks for the time of return to their source.

Mingling with both happy and unhappy people,
in every gathering, I sang my lament.

Every one became my friend
from their own idea of me,
and no one sought out my inner secrets.

My heart's secret is not far from my sung
  lament,
yet eyes and ears lack the spiritual light
to illuminate them.

The body is not veiled from the soul,
nor the soul from the body—
yet no one is taught to see the soul.

As I puckered up, Kemal placed the *ney* on the tip of my lips, just so. I huffed and I puffed into the shaft of the coy *ney*. Nothing. Baba chuckled as I handed the hollow baton back and forth with Kemal. Still, nothing.

"Zemzem, in order to play the *ney*, you must have the fire of love in your belly, not just wind," Baba said, putting on his glasses to read more verses from the opening of Rumi's masterpiece:

The cry of the ney *is fire, not wind—*
whoever lacks this fire is nothing.

It's the fire of love that makes the ney's *songs burn,*
and the fervor of love that makes wine sparkle.

The ney *is a companion to whomever*
has been separated from a friend,
and torn the veils covering the truth from us.

Who ever saw a poison and antidote like the ney?
Who ever saw a confidant and longing lover like the ney?

The ney *sings of the path flooded with blood,*
and relates stories of Majnun's love.

This level of understanding is only confided
to those who have lost all their senses.
The tongue has no client save for the ear.

In our sorrowful longing, every day feels untimely,
for our days travel hand in hand
with the burning flames of love.

If the days are gone, I am not afraid to tell them: go ahead!
Yet please stay with me, you who are perfect in purity.

High from all the futile puffing, I took a break to restore my oxygen level before returning to trying to attain the unattainable on the *ney*. A chronic perfectionist, I was relieved to be an utter disaster on the reed flute—and I was glad I could provide Baba with some amusement, as he chuckled at me from the corner and returned to reading Rumi.

DANCING IN THE SKY

When that candle has becomes joy-increasing,
you'll come dancing like those
with fluttering hearts like butterflies.

When your soul departs,
your body won't shake.
When your soul returns,
you'll rise from the grave!

When the ecstatic clamor of whirling
washes over the mountain,
O heavy mountain,
you'll be flattened by the sound!

This spring breeze is inviting
the golden branch to dance.

How can a speck of dust remain at rest,
when the sun is dancing in the sky?

Both fire and smoke have become twisted
from the blazing fire of the soul—increasing one's face.

O moon, my obsession, bodiless spirit—
you are my sweet amusement,
and trial of affliction.

Sometimes we become short, sometimes long—
with a shadow in the form of a phoenix.

From the lips of the beloved, we become drunk—
weepy and wasted like the reed flute.

We're gliding on the wind like straw,
in a parade pulled by amber.

O my heart, we're drunk on our own blood like gnats,
and cooked in the cauldron of a heartsick liver.

In private, shouting in ecstasy: "O Him!"
And in public, crying out: "O Living One!"

In appearance, we're worthless slaves—
in secret, we possess the attribute of the one divinity.

This is the gift of the king, Shams of Tabriz—
without pride but with the power of the Almighty.

TOLERANCE

◆

When Rumi wandered west as a ten-year-old boy with his family on the Silk Road routes connecting Central Asia to Anatolia and the Mediterranean Sea, it was not only goods—like silks and spices—they saw being traded, but religious, spiritual, and philosophical ideas, too. Rumi was fully immersed in the religious and cultural diversity of Central Asia and the Middle East in the thirteenth century, as a result of encountering a number of diverse cultures and different faiths as his family migrated in search of safety and security. In Rumi's poetry, he mentions a variety of spiritual traditions and practices with great respect and openhearted tolerance.

> *This filled-to-the-brim world is full of Jesus.*
> *The wares of the Antichrist will never find space in this world.*
> *There will never be room for the bitter, salty water*
>   *of a dark heart,*
> *because the canteen of the world is full of pure water.*

Along the Silk Road, Rumi would have encountered pagan, Zoroastrian, Manichaean, and Buddhist ideas, in addition to seeing many mosques, churches, and sectarian ritual processions. In his poetry, Rumi references Abrahamic prophets, Zoroastrian ritual dress, Manichaean paintings, and Buddhist icons. Rumi's compassionate, virtuous, and humble manner earned him the respect of local Muslims, Jews, and Christians alike.

Be careful, don't say: "There aren't any real travelers
  on the way.
There aren't any with the qualities of Jesus or the traceless."
Since you aren't an intimate of the secrets,
you've assumed others are not too.

YOUR FACE

If one pore of your face revealed itself,
not a dervish cloak nor a Christian belt
  would remain upon the earth.

The moment you reveal your face
  to someone from the two worlds,
they're set ablaze and have no business
  other than longing for you.

If you throw the veil from that beautiful face,
no traces remain of the faces of the sun and moon.

You put to sleep those who burn with love,
so no one is privy to the secrets save for you.

Some Muslim mystics today speak about different religions occupying different chambers of the heart; they are all one, and united in their essence, but occupying separate, connected rooms. Rumi's verses invoke many of the Biblical prophets, as well as Mary, the mother of Jesus, who appears in more verses of the Qur'an than the Bible.

In this fire, I have seen a world
in which every atom is a breath of Jesus.

In the Qur'an, Mary becomes pregnant with Jesus through immaculate conception, and Jesus is called the "Messiah" who will return to preside over the Day of Judgment. Jesus also raises the dead and heals the disabled and sick. In Rumi's poetry, Jesus and the other prophets embody wisdom and spiritual insight and give mystic lessons to heal the human heart. As al-Ghazali wrote, "In general, then, the prophets (Peace be upon them!) are the physicians for treating the maladies of hearts."

In the garden, everyone is drinking
the pure wine of God—
yet none among them has a throat.

The trees in the garden are wonderful,
as they are virginal yet pregnant,
like Mary who has neither a lover nor husband.

In Rumi's time, many Muslims held critical judgments about the wine-drinking, pork eating, and religious processions of Greek and Armenian Christians, which made Rumi and Shams's time spent in the Christian neighborhoods particularly unusual. Of course, Christian neighborhoods in cities like Baghdad and Damascus were where alcohol was freely available, as monks tended to the vineyards and brewed wine. Rumi and Shams were very familiar with the tavern district, and Rumi spent a great deal of time conversing with members of the Greek, Armenian, and Jewish communities.

JOHN THE BAPTIST'S MOTHER

John the Baptist's mother came to Mary in secret
before her childbearing and said to her:

"I am certain you are carrying a King—
a Lord of Constancy and Apostle of Consciousness.

When I spoke with you before face-to-face,
the baby in my womb prostrated toward you—
you who are all comprehension!

This fetus prostrated to that fetus,
and my body suffered pain from this prostration."

Mary told her: "I too felt within me
a prostration from the child in my womb."

Rumi drew inspiration for his poetic depiction of these prophetic figures from the Qur'an. As Shams explained, "The prophets are always those who accept and confirm each other. And their words are always words that explain and complete each other." Rumi incorporates Noah, Abraham, Adam, Isaac, Ishmael, Jacob, Joseph, Solomon, Moses, Aaron, Elijah, Elisha, Jonah, David, Job, John the Baptist, Jesus, and the Prophet Muhammad into his verses in his exploration of deep spiritual truths and prophetic consciousness.

If you make my face beautiful, my beauty will be yours.
If you grip me like a rod, I'll be your staff of Moses too.
And if you tear me to pieces, in pain, I'll be your Job.
O Joseph of the era, I will be your Jacob.

To understand Rumi's universalist vision, it is helpful to contemplate his verses that reach beyond faith to point toward another realm of being and worshipping. While these verses may seem almost heretical at first glance, Rumi is, in fact, capturing the essence of devotion and love of the divine apart from rigid notions of religion or belief.

> *Beyond unbelief and Islam, there is a desert.*
> *For us there is a yearning in the midst of that expanse.*
> *The gnostic who reaches that place will prostrate.*
> *There is neither unbelief nor Islam nor any "there"*
>   *in that place.*

For Rumi, a mystic is not just a Muslim—but a lover who has gone beyond the narrow confines of religious identification. In Rumi's poetic articulations, the lover does not subscribe to a certain Islamic school of jurisprudence or fixate on religious law. A lover goes beyond intellect to drown completely in the ocean of love.

> *Know truly the lover: he isn't a Muslim.*
> *In the religion of love, there's neither unbelief nor faith.*
> *In love, there's neither body nor intellect nor heart nor soul.*
> *Anyone not like this—is not a lover.*

WHO IS SEEKING?

> *The seeking of the lovers doesn't come from themselves,*
> *as there is no seeker but him.*

> *This world and that world are one essence—*
> *in reality, there's no truth, unbelief, religion, or faith.*

O you, your breath is like the breath of Jesus.
Don't breathe from a distance!
I am the admirer of the one
who's not far-thinking.

If you say: "I'll go behind"—don't go!
There is no behind.
If you say, "I'll go ahead"—no!
There is no way ahead.

Open your hand,
and grab the hem of
your own cloak.
There's no dressing
for this wound
except this garment.

All good and bad qualities are within a dervish.
Whoever is not like this—
is not a dervish.

Whoever has gone beyond place,
her place is the heart—
for such a heart,
there's no place in the world.

DO NOT DESPAIR

Do not despair, my soul,
for hope has come and manifested itself.
The hope of all souls has come,
arriving from the unseen.

Do not despair, though Mary has slipped from your hands,
for the light which drew Jesus to heaven has come.

Do not despair, my soul,
in the darkness of this prison,
for the king who freed Joseph
from prison has come.

Jacob has emerged from the veil of concealment,
and Joseph who tore Zulaykha's veil has come.

O you, who've been crying out from night until dawn:
"O Lord! O Lord!"
Mercy has heard your "O Lord! O Lord!" and come.

O pain which has grown old, rejoice—
for the cure has come!
O fastened lock, open—
for the key has come!

O you, who've fasted from the table on high,
break your fast with joy,
for the first day of the holiday feast has come.

Now be silent, be silent—
for because of the divine command "Be!"
the silence of bewilderment has become
greater than all speech.

In his poetry, Rumi illustrates the battle a spiritual wayfarer
has with his ego with the story of Moses and Pharaoh in the
Qur'an. In Sufism, Pharaoh tends to represent the desires and

qualities of the ego—arrogance and the desire to oppress and acquire. He is attached to this world of dust and is determined to dominate it. Pharaoh embodies the negative qualities that a seeker on the path of truth must obliterate within his own heart to taste sweet union with the divine.

> *Such a grace that is flowing like the Nile*
> *turns into blood for us,*
> *since we are like Pharaoh.*

Divine love has the power to obliterate us. According to Rumi, we all have Moses and Pharaoh inside of us. Sufis to this day invoke the figures of Moses and Pharaoh to encourage dervishes on the mystic path to break free from the imprisoning impulses of the self and seek true liberation. Rumi even compares mystics to the ancient Israelites led by Moses: "The gnostics are always safe, because they have passed through a sea of blood." Love has the power to slay us and save us.

> *This torturing love is two-faced,*
> *just like the Nile was water to its favorite tribe,*
> *and murderous to the rest.*

Rumi references Moses more than any other prophet in his masterpiece, *The Masnavi*. In the Quranic account, similar to the Biblical account, God says to Moses: "Moses, it is me, your Lord. Remove your sandals, for you are in the sacred valley of Tuwa. I myself have chosen you; so listen closely to what is revealed. Truly, I am God; there is no god but I; therefore serve me, and perform the prayer of my remembrance." Moses removes his worldly attachments to step into the divine presence. In the burning bush Rumi gleans the fire of love that attracts a spiritual seeker and initiates him into the sacred realm.

> *O my Moses, you went to Mount Sinai,*
> *and departed from my inner and outer states.*
> *You've never become cold from those warmths.*
> *How could you become cold,*
>   *when you've left for divine warmth?*

Moses not only embodies and typifies the mystic journey—he also transmits the light of prophecy. One of Moses's miracles in the Qur'an is that his arm was able to spread white light. As the Qur'an states, "And he drew forth his hand, and lo! It was white for the beholders." In Sufism, mystic knowledge is conceptualized as a vision of light. As Rumi writes, "O light of Moses, and the Mountain of Sinai, that is who you are!" In the eternal fire of love, as epitomized by the burning bush, a mystic heart can never grow cold.

I SAW HIM

> *I saw the good and beautiful-faced king—*
> *that eye and lamp of the chest!*
> *That intimate and consoler of the heart!*
> *That soul-increasing soul and world!*
>
> *The one who gives intellect to intellect and purity to purity.*
> *The idol of worship for the heavens and moon.*
> *The prayer direction of the souls of the saints.*
>
> *Every part of me was crying out separately:*
> *"Thanks and thanksgiving be to God!"*

When Moses suddenly saw the light
of the burning bush, he said:
"From seeking and searching I've been delivered,
for I've found this gift!"

God said: "O Moses, leave traveling behind!
Throw down that staff!"

At once, Moses cast out from his heart
friends, neighbors, and kin.

This is the essence of "Remove your sandals,"
and "Cut off your love from the two worlds!"

In the heart of hearts, nothing fits but him.
The heart knows the jealousy of the prophets.

God said: "O Moses, what do you have
    in the palm of your hand?"
Moses answered: "My staff for the path."

God said: "Cast down the staff from your hands,
and behold the marvels of heaven!"

Moses threw down the staff,
and it became a serpent.
When he saw the serpent, he fled.

God said: "Take it, and I'll make it your staff again."

From your enemy, I'll make you a heart companion—
I'll transform your foe into your crutch.

Then you'll know that kind and faithful friends
come only from my loving grace.

When we give pain to your hands and feet,
your hands and feet become like serpents in your eyes.

O hand, seize anyone other than us!
O foot, seek only the finish line!

Flee not from difficulties—
for wherever there is suffering,
there is a path to the cure.

No one has ever fled from suffering,
without receiving a foul-smelling penalty in return.

So flee from the bait—
that is the place of fear.
Leave fear of places
to the anxious intellect.

Shams of Tabriz has shown his tenderness,
but when he went away—
he took it with him.

The prophet Joseph in Rumi's poetry is the embodiment of beauty. He is described in the Qur'an as so handsome that Egyptian women in his presence, distracted by his beauty, accidentally cut their hands with their kitchen knives while staring at him. One woman, named Zulaykha, was especially infatuated with him. In his poetry, Rumi turns her lust for Joseph and his escape from her desire into a lesson about leaving the world behind.

> *O moon, you are the atonement for every kind of sin.*
> *No, you are the rope for Joseph in the soul of the well.*
> *No, rather, you are the guide on the path.*
> *You are the key to a thousand suns, O moon.*

Rumi identified closely with Joseph's father, Jacob, who in the Qur'an becomes so distressed by Joseph's disappearance and the evil plot of his jealous brothers that he becomes blind. Similarly, murder rumors had swirled about Shams, who had mysteriously disappeared from Konya one night and was never seen or heard from again. For Rumi, Joseph was a reminder of Shams, with whom he yearned to be reunited. As Rumi wrote, "O Joseph of the soul, ask about the state of Jacob. And, o generous soul, ask about the suffering of Jacob!" Jacob was the symbol of Rumi himself—the longing spiritual lover lamenting the loss of his mystic beloved.

> *The moment when the scent of your shirt arrives—*
> *   what will I do?*
> *The circling sky will tear its robe in ecstasy!*
> *Where is that fine-scented shirt of Joseph?*
> *Today, it will take the scent of your shirt.*

In the Qur'an, when Joseph reveals his true identity to his brothers, he has his shirt sent back with them to Jacob, whose sight miraculously heals when he recognizes the scent of his missing son. Jacob's transformation, from sorrowful yearning over the perceived loss of his beloved son to ecstatic union upon news of Joseph's return, served for Rumi as hope and inspiration for his aching heart.

RUN AWAY

Although Zulaykha had closed all the doors,
Joseph was still able to find a way out,
because he was restless to leave.

As the door was opened to him,
the way out became clear—
because he trusted in God,
he escaped.

Though the escapeway out of this world isn't visible,
you should run away like Joseph—
even though fleeing at first may appear in vain.

When you run, the locks will all open,
and the exit will appear—
if your heart has a dwelling place
in the spacelessness of the other world.

You have come to this world only to be given a test,
but do you see at all the path you came from?

You have indeed come from a place that is your homeland,
but do you know the way you got here? No!

If you don't know, you shouldn't say there is no way out,
because this world has led us astray and we will go out of it.

Rumi also includes the excessive suffering of the prophet Job in his poetry. In the Qur'an, the prophet Job models patient forbearance: "Affliction has seized me, but you are the most

merciful of the merciful." Job represents the suffering of the
spiritual seeker on the mystic path, whose healing comes in the
form of divine love.

> *Be happy, all you students: the requested one has come!*
> *Shout, all you lovers, for the beloved has come!*
> *That healing for the afflictions of Job has come!*
> *That Joseph of a hundred thousand Jacobs has come.*

In the Qur'an, despite all his trials and tribulations, Job
continues to worship God through daily prayer, and in his un-
shakable gratitude, he counts his blessings. Eventually, Job's
suffering is lifted and God blesses him with wealth, ease, and
many generations of descendants. As a verse in the Qur'an says:
"Surely with difficulty comes ease."

> *O you, who are Joseph to me, as if I am Jacob.*
> *O you, who are the health of the body to me, as if I am Job.*
> *How can I be anyone myself,*
>   *since you are the beloved of everyone?*
> *I keep clapping my hands, so you can stomp*
>   *your feet and dance.*

As in the Bible, Adam is the father of humanity in the Qur'an.
For Rumi, Adam was the astrolabe of the exalted attributes of
God; everything that appeared in Adam was a reflection of the
divine, like the reflection of the moon in a stream. Rumi writes,
"We have all been parts of Adam. We have heard those mel-
odies in paradise." He suggests that we have all already, in a
sense, been in paradise, as according to Islamic theology we all
started life in a state of purity and innocence. The mystic path is

a way to return to our original nature, our blank simplicity, and restore the natural harmony of our soul to align with the divine.

> *We will not give your dust even for the water of Zamzam.*
> *We will not receive happiness or give away any of this longing.*
> *This face of yours is the fortune of humanity.*
> *We will not give the splendor of your face even to Adam.*

Zamzam is the holy well at Mecca, which Muslims believe is filled with pure, healing water. It was revealed to Hajar, the second wife of Abraham and mother of Ishmael, who was thirsty and crying out for water. Rumi says he would not trade a speck of dust from the divine for anything in this world—not even the holiest water in Islam or happiness itself.

Rumi also writes about the prophet Solomon, whose mighty army of men, birds, and genies in the Qur'an ignites awe in even the smallest ants. Solomon appears in many medieval Persian poems. Solomon was able to understand the languages of various animals, such as birds and even ants. In the Qur'an, Solomon and his army enter a valley of ants. A female ant warns the other ants to run back to their shelters so Solomon does not crush them underfoot. Solomon understands her cry and avoids stepping on their colony.

> *We are lovers of love, but a Muslim is different.*
> *We are weak ants, but Solomon is different.*
> *Ask us about our pale cheeks and destroyed livers.*
> *The bazaar of the butchers is different.*

The ants are weak and vulnerable as opposed to the might of Solomon the king. But Rumi seems to sarcastically suggest that the ants, like dervish lovers, are actually more pure and powerful than the king or more orthodox Muslims, as their "weakness" is actually a sign of their exalted state of humility and spiritual poverty: in annihilating their selves, dervishes become small but mighty. In fact, "weakness" is one of the stations on the mystic path toward complete spiritual poverty—being empty of all ego, ambition, and desire.

> *O heart, pass away from love, beloved, and from friend.*
> *If you are sharp-sighted, bind the Zoroastrian's cord belt*
>   *around all three.*
> *Go to the crucible of nonexistence and don't have fear,*
> *for this poverty is free from stranger and friend.*

Rumi weaves the prophet Zoroaster and Zoroastrian symbols through his poetry. In Zoroastrianism, the religion that follows the Persian prophet Zoroaster, followers wear a cord that is knotted three times to remind them to practice good words, good thoughts, and good deeds. Rumi frames the mystic emphasis on love, friend, and beloved as a heretical trinity that should be bound with the belt of Zoroastrianism—a symbol of unbelief itself! Release yourself, Rumi provocatively implores the mystic, even from attachment to mystical concepts—for true enlightenment and union are detached from all concepts, ideas, and relations!

> *You should know that insight based on reason*
> *is only a vestibule one passes through—*
> *even Plato says the main house is in the outer world.*

The Greek philosopher Plato also appears in Rumi's poetry—as a great sage. In Rumi's day, Neoplatonic thought, which framed knowledge as a mystical ascension of illumination, was popular and influential in a variety of spiritual paths and religious traditions. Rumi reportedly not only frequently visited Plato's monastery nearby but also took retreats there among monks from the Byzantine Empire and Europe.

THE MOON IN MY EYES

I keep seeing a moon in my eyes from outside my eyes—
but my eyes have not seen him,
nor my ears heard of him.

I have seen neither tongue, nor soul, nor heart
  except in selflessness,
from the moment I first stole a glance at that face.

If Plato had seen the beauty and virtue of that moon,
he would've become crazier and more distraught than me!

Preexistence is the mirror of time, and temporality
  the mirror of preexistence.
In that mirror, these two are intertwined—
like his two curls.

Beyond the senses is a cloud—whose rain is all soul.
What rains have showered blessings like sugar
on the dust of his body!

The moon-faced beauties of heaven have seen
the reflection of his face.
Ashamed at his beauty,
they scratch at the napes of their necks
in awe and hesitation.

Eternity-without-beginning grasped the hand
  of eternity-without-end,
and they reached the palace of that moon.
Jealousy looked at the two and laughed.

"Around his palace, what lions have come from jealousy—
roaring for the blood of the ones who risk
  their lives and the sincere."

Suddenly, these words leapt from my lips:
  "Who is that king?"
"Shams al-Din, the king of Tabriz."
From this answer, the passion in my blood
  began to boil.

Religious identity in Seljuk-ruled Anatolia was multifaceted and accommodating. Christians and Muslims in Anatolia in Rumi's time had "shared saints." For example, Christians venerated the Christian saint Amphilochius of Iconium, and Muslims paid their respects at the same place to Plato the philosopher. Today in Turkey, Christians and Muslims alike visit the House of Virgin Mary in Izmir out of their shared reverence for the mother of Jesus.

The chief of the monks of Plato's monastery—an old and well-educated religious authority to whom Christians came from all over to seek knowledge and guidance—recounted one of Rumi's visits to this sacred site. He recalled:

One day Mowlana [Rumi] came to Plato's Monastery which stands at the foot of a mountain, and he went into the cave from which cold water flows forth. He set off to penetrate to the very end of the cave. I waited outside the cave watching to see what would happen. Mowlana sat in the middle of the cold water for seven days and nights. After that, filled with passionate excitement, he came outside and departed. Truly, there was no trace of change whatsoever in his blessed body.

The monk watched in astonishment as Rumi performed the miraculous feat of meditating for seven days in cold water. The monk also swore that "What I have read about the person of the Messiah and in the sacred books of Abraham and Moses, as well as what I have seen in the histories of the ancestors concerning the magnitude of the austerities of the prophets—the very same, and even more, was in Mowlana."[6]

Centuries before Rumi lived, ancient philosophical ideas from Greece had already been integrated into classical Islamic thought and philosophy. The ruling Rum Seljuks had an explicit interest in philosophy. In the twelfth century, Suhrawardi, a Persian Muslim philosopher who was the founder of the Philosophy of Illumination and influenced by Plato, conceptualized the "light" as a divine source of knowledge. In Suhrawardi's esoteric interpretation of the pre-Islamic *Persian Book of Kings*, kingly figures like Kay-Khosraw are understood to be manifestations of divine light. Suhrawardi even put the Persian prophet Zoroaster and legends like Kay-Khosraw in conversation with Plato.

Whoso questions the truth of this—whosoever is unconvinced by the proof—let him engage in mystical disciplines and service to those visionaries, that perchance he will, as one dazzled by the thunderbolt, see the light blazing in the Kingdom of Power and will witness the heavenly essences and lights that Hermes and Plato beheld. He will see the spiritual luminaries, the wellsprings of kingly splendor and wisdom that Zoroaster told of, and that which the good and blessed king Kay-Khosraw un-expectedly beheld in a flash. All the sages of Persia were agreed thereon. . . . These are the lights to which Emped-ocles and others alluded.[7]

Suhrawardi thought that this divine light that shone through Persian history united these different philosophical and spiritual traditions. Thus, during Rumi's era, many phi-losophers and mystics were engaged in exploring the spiritual threads that seemed to unite different traditions—including pre-Islamic philosophers and sages.

Rumi's early migrations along the Silk Road and the diverse population of Konya likely shaped his tolerant views regarding people from different religions, races, and classes. As Rumi ex-plained, all beings are like a bunch of grapes—if squeezed to-gether, no difference or separation remains. Rumi emphasized that when our gaze is on goodness, loving kindness, and toler-ance, then all divisions fall away.

Where there is kindness, be it in peace or war—
and if the act is goodness, be it prayers or quarrel—
if a man is accepted, be he Byzantine or Zanzibari,
surrender and forgive you must—
not with pride or a heart of stone.

Such divisions, of course, are just manifestations of earthly affairs and egotistic identifications. In his poetry, Rumi cau-tions against burdening the soul with earthly affairs. He rec-ommends curbing bodily pleasure and instead tending to the soul—keeping it fenced off from the problems of the world. In his poetry, Jesus becomes a metaphor for the soul, and his don-key a symbol of the body.

THE SYRUP OF LOVE

What is justice? To water the trees.
What is injustice? To water the thorns.

To do justice is to grant everything grace,
appropriate to its place.
Not to water every root,
just because it's a watersucker.

What is injustice? To inappropriately grant something,
which leads to nothing but disaster.

Endow your soul and reason with the grace of truth—
lose your nature of being
full of afflictions and complications.

Let your body shoulder the burden
 of aggravating anxieties—
don't bother your heart and soul with worldly affairs.

You have put an overloaded burden on Jesus,
while his donkey is frolicking in the meadow.

It's not proper to put kohl on your ears,
nor demand the body perform the job of the heart.

If you're moved by the heart,
play hard to get instead of indulging humiliation!
And if you're ruled by the body,
don't drink from the syrup of love—
and taste the hemlock instead!

In 1273, when Rumi died at sixty-six years old, his funeral was attended by Muslims, Christians, and Jews. Persians, Arabs, Greeks, and Turks participated in his funeral procession. Their lamentations melted together as one as mystic music played and dervishes whirled alongside his coffin to his tomb. Imams, rabbis, and priests carrying the Qur'an, the Torah, and the Gospels joined in the procession to pay their respects. Rumi had spent his life trying to polish the mirror of his heart to receive and reflect the divine essence—to shine the light of love into all corners of the earth. People of different faiths saw their own prophets and traditions reflected in his loving heart, emptied of all selfhood.

FROM MY GRAVE

If wheat sprouts from my grave,
and you bake bread from it,
drunkenness will abound!

The dough and the baker
will become insane,
and the oven will sing
ecstatic verses like a drunk.

If you make a pilgrimage to my grave,
its burial mound will shake
and get you dancing!

Don't come to my tomb
without a tambourine, brother,
since you wouldn't be full of sorrow

at the banquet of God.
My once chattering chin
is now sleeping in the grave,
but my mouth is still feasting on opium
and sweets of the beloved.

Tear a piece from that funeral shroud,
and bind it to your chest.
From deep in your soul,
open the door of a tavern.

From every direction, the sound of war roars,
and the harps of the drunkards sing.
From every action,
more action is inevitably born.

Truth has created me from the wine of love.
Even if death grinds me down,
I am still that same love.

I am drunkenness and my origin is the wine of love.
Tell me: what comes from wine except drunkenness?

My soul will fly without a moment's hesitation
to the heavenly home of the spirit of Shams al-Din of Tabriz.

* * *

I am obliterated in God, and God is absorbed in me.
Why do you look in all directions?
Look in the soul.

One afternoon, while snacking on a giant fruit plate and baklava with his dervishes, Baba gave us a short talk on the connectedness of different religious traditions.

"Sufism, you see, is not any different from the mysticism found in any other religion: there is only one river, yet a river may flow through more than one country. Similar to how a country cannot claim a river as their own if the river flows through many different countries, so too are the paths of mysticism, which all go toward experiencing the divine," Baba said.

It was Rumi, he said, who gave full expression to the source of all religions and spiritual paths—the way of love—which flows through many cultures and traditions.

As I looked at the serene expressions on the faces of my Turkish brothers—dry cleaners, doctors, and artists—I paused and reflected on the mystical events that had led me to my forty-day retreat in that special spiritual corner of Istanbul.

Baba elucidated the ways in which Rumi embodied the noble qualities of the holy hearts in all the sacred traditions—the peace and compassion of Buddha, the beauty and insight of Joseph, the courage and righteousness of Moses, the wisdom and power of Solomon, the love and healing of Jesus, and the light and clarity of the Prophet Muhammad, peace be upon them all.

"Their qualities are not just part of us, but the very essence of our own human nature," Baba said, demonstrating how the tolerance of Rumi's vision lives on in the whirling dervishes who follow in his path today.

ANNIHILATION

For a dervish, nonexistence is the highest level. The "freed ones" are the dervishes who have annihilated their egos, detached from the world, and cast off self-centered preoccupation. A Sufi shaykh once said to me, "The price of being a dervish is one's whole life." The mystic path is a lifelong endeavor that requires one's whole being. Each breath is sacrificed to sensing and connecting with divine love and extinguishing one's self through selfless service to one's loved ones, friends, and communities.

> *If you step on the way, the way will be opened to you.*
> *And if you become nonexistent, you'll be led to existence.*
> *If you become humble, you won't be contained in the*
>   *cosmos—*
> *and then you'll be shown to yourself without yourself.*

A Sufi relinquishes her vain desires and delusions of the self—to become well-pleasing to the beloved and unveil her own true essence. The fire of love in her heart burns her ego to ash. In sacrificing the demands of her commanding self, she gains mystic knowledge. As Rumi explains, progress on the mystic path enables us to change our "I see not" to "I see," and our "I don't know"s to "I know."

I became annihilated,
and all the components of my body

flew to the heavens,
since my first homeland was in the heavens.
They're drunk and delighted there,
and they're all wine worshippers in that invisible realm—
in contrast to the misery and prison I'm in.

For Rumi, the material world and the self are a prison and mirage. As the Qur'an says, "All that is upon the earth will disappear, but the face of your Lord will endure, full of majesty and splendor."

Someone said: "In the whole world, there is no dervish,
and if there is a dervish, that dervish is not!"

Grasping at the self, we mistakenly think that it is our anchor in the world. We cling to the self like a life raft in the ever-changing and unknowable circumstances of our days. On the one hand, the self gives us a sense of control; on the other hand, it is never satisfied. A dervish free from selfhood transcends the delusions and afflictions of the limited mind and distracted heart.

Every dervish shattered of self
(so you don't suspect he thinks delusional things)—
the tent camp of that one of good faith
is better than existence, location, and the whole world.

When a dervish purifies his heart from negative characteristics and annihilates the ego, then only the love, compassion, mercy, guidance, wisdom, and will of the divine remain. Shatter the idol of ego, Rumi encourages us, and be free! Why do we choose to live under the veil of opinions—our lives driven by judgments and the illusion of selfhood—instead of pursuing with passion the everlasting divine reality?

> *I went to the doctor and said: "O seeing one!*
> *For the love-fallen one, what do you prescribe?"*
> *He prescribed renunciation of personal attributes*
>   *and the annihilation of my being—*
> *which means: Come out from all that exists!*

Without selfhood, a dervish heart melts into a blissful state of consciousness—a peaceful yet ecstatic way of being in the world. Such ecstasy may manifest in an intoxicated manner or be veiled in the sobriety of humility. Freed from negative thoughts, markers of identity, and habitual preoccupations, a dervish ceases to exist! As Rumi says, the business of true religion is nothing but bewilderment—so sell your cleverness and buy bewilderment instead!

> *I am pure and clear, but also the muddy dregs of wine.*
> *I'm a spiritual master and old man, but also a small child.*
> *If I die, don't say about me: "He died."*
> *Say I was dead, I became alive—*
>   *and then the friend took me.*

A dervish can possess the wisdom of a great master, and also the open mind and wonder of a child. The end of the mystic path is a return to the beginning. Who can know if the "annihilation" of the ego is a spiritual death enacted by the dervish, or a blessed act of grace—an experience of being "taken" by the beloved?

I died from the longing of love.
Breathe on me for a moment,
so I can live from that one moment forever.
You said: in union, we'll be intimate friends.
Really—where, with whom, and in what place?

Sufis often repeat, "He who knows himself knows his Lord." However, self-realization is not the final goal. On the contrary, the illusory ego and desires must be abandoned and the will and guiding hand of God sought if a dervish is to awaken from the slumber of self-centered obsession to the bewildering and beautiful reality of the divine. As Rumi wrote, "Because non-existence is the highest stage, dervishes take precedence over everyone."

Since I've flung the crown of egotism
  from my head, behold:
I've tightened my belt in service to you.
I've wept a lot, but separation just laughed.
Now it's time for it to weep and me to laugh!

How liberating to throw off the crown of egotism—to be free from the pretense and shackles of the self! The dethronement of the ego is a necessary step on the mystic path. Rumi suggests that in our separation from the beloved, we are plunged into sorrow—but when we feel union with the divine, we can look back and laugh at our folly in ever having perceived separation! For a dervish who has achieved this station, she draws her breath only for the sake of the divine.

HOMELESS

"It's better to fall prey than to pray,"
love whispers softly in my ear.

"Make a fool of yourself over me,
and pride yourself on me.
Give up shining like the sun,
and become a speck instead.

Become homeless and reside at my door.
Don't claim to be a candle,
but instead turn into a moth.

Then you'll sense the flavor of life,
which is to discover the sultanate
hidden in servitude."

There are different types and levels of annihilation—a dervish can "annihilate" her self in her shaykh, or in the founding shaykh of her Sufi order, or in the Prophet Muhammad, or in God so that no individual will remain. Usually, a dervish will experience annihilation in that specific order, but not always. As stated in the Qur'an, "What is with you will vanish, and what is with God will endure." To describe this phenomenon, Sufis point to Hadith Qudsi in the Islamic tradition, in which God says:

When I love him, I am his hearing with which he hears, his seeing with which he sees, his hand with which he strikes and his foot with which he walks. Were he to ask something of Me, I would surely give it to him, and were he to ask Me for refuge, I would surely grant him it.

A Sufi empties himself like a vessel to be filled with the divine presence. As Shams explained, "When someone's [self] and his devil, that is, his evil character dies, or when he is purified of blameworthy attributes and characteristics, he attains God." But he was careful to point out that "no one can attain God's divine essence; they can reach only to the light of His path."

> I am faded in God and God is all mine!
> Don't go looking for him in all directions,
>   for he's within my soul.
> I am sultan, so if I say someone else is my sultan—
>   I am mistaken.

Eventually on the dervish path, spiritual seeking is replaced with mystic abiding. At that stage, a dervish no longer wanders in search of mystic knowledge but can rest in the divine presence, which she finds within her own heart and soul. She has found the kingdom within. She sets up residence in the palace of her being: instead of wandering across foreign deserts, she goes exploring the heart chambers where the beloved's secret treasures are hidden. She has become a servant in the palace of the beloved. She has answered love's call to annihilate herself and gained a special place in the kingdom of the heart.

ONCE AGAIN

> Once again, we've walked away
>   from heart, intellect, and soul.
> The friend came among us,
> and we disappeared.
>
> We've turned our faces from annihilation,
> and woven ourselves into subsistence.

We've found the traceless,
and from the traces risen.

We stirred dust in the ocean
and smoke in the nine spheres,
rising above time, the earth, and heavens.

Look out—the drunkards have come!
Open the way!
No, I said that wrong—
for we've been liberated
from the way and its wardens.

The fire of the soul
flames out of the earthly body.

Shouts from the heart rise up,
and like a shout,
we rise up too.

Let us say fewer words,
for if we speak,
few understand.

Pour more wine,
for we've been conversing
with moderate drinkers.

Existence is for women—
nonexistence is the work of men.

Thanks be to God,
for we have risen
as champions in nonexistence!

When immolated in the fire of love, existence and nonexistence don't even make sense. There is no duality or division—no life or death, no consciousness or unconsciousness—in the ocean of love. Rumi describes such a spiritual state as: "That place where I was not existence or location—where I was not me or the universe."

> We tie the garments of existence on nonexistence.
> We laugh at two-faced being and nonbeing.
> Playfully and carelessly, we've cut the ropes,
> and uprooted the tent of patience from the sky.

With the self extinguished, the dervish becomes freed from both existence and nonexistence—playfully present to the "now" without expectation or understanding. As Shams wrote, "You love yourself and find fault with the mirror. Because the one who loves his or her own ego respects only the ego, while the one who loves the mirror, gives up both ego and mirror." Eventually, there is no self or other, no lover or beloved—there is nothing but truth and the ultimate reality. With the self extinguished, the dervish does not know where he ends and his mystic master or divine beloved begins.

> I am not me, and you are not you, and you are not me.
> I am also me, and you are also you, and you are me too.
> O idol of Khotan, with you I am such that
> I'm confused if I am you or you are me!

The idol of Khotan refers to a Silk Road city in Xinjiang (East Turkestan) in western China, inhabited by Turkic tribes, that was legendary for its prized musk, beautiful inhabitants, and Manichaean images. Shams was Rumi's idol—in whom he lost himself completely. A lover who loses her life in love demonstrates that annihilation is the principle and essence of loving.

THE BELOVED'S SAKE

There was a lover who would name
all he'd done for his beloved,
and how he'd served her.

"I did this for the sake of that," the lover bragged,
as if hit by arrows and spearheads
on the battlefield.

"My wealth, my might, and my reputation are all gone.
From loving you, I've suffered many misfortunes.
No morning found me asleep or in laughter—
no evening found me safe and sound."

The lover enumerated in detail all the bitterness
and pain he'd experienced in love.

He didn't mean to guilt-trip his beloved—
he just wanted to prove his genuine love.

A hint is enough for reasonable people to understand,
but lovers long for much more to quench their thirst for love.

There was a fire in this lover,
who knew not what it was,
but its heat made him weep like a candle.

"You have done all this—it's true!
Yet listen carefully to me,
and grasp my point well," the beloved replied.

"You haven't done the principle of the principles
*   of friendship and love—*
all you've done is tangential," the beloved continued.

"Tell me what the principle is,"
the lover said.

"The principle is to die and become nothing,"
said the beloved.

"Although you've done all those things,
you're still alive and not yet dead—
if you're willing to lose your life in love,
O friend, then let yourself die!"

Instantly, the lover passed out
and gave up his life,
losing his cheerful, laughing head
like a flower.

In his own exalted spiritual rank, Rumi believed that nothing was really under his command—not even his own breath. He saw all manifestations—even the Mongol destruction of the Islamic world—as divinely ordained. Rumi went wherever the invisible hand moved him. In his poetry, Rumi often compares the invisible force controlling his movements to games played on fields and matches on game boards.

You think I'm in charge of myself?
Or that even one breath I inhale or exhale is by my command?
I'm like a pen in the grip of my calligrapher.
I'm like a ball—slave to the master of the polo mallet.

Rumi repeatedly paints himself as a polo ball struck on the playing field of love. Many Persian lyric poets drew upon polo as an image for the helplessness and submission of the lover to the beloved. The faithful lover is rebuffed time and time again.

From the moment I first knew you through love,
so many secret games of backgammon I've played with you—
all of which I've lost.
Because of your drunken and graceful gait
*   through the tent of my heart,*
I've emptied the whole tent for your sake alone.

Rumi was also fond of employing the imagery of chess and backgammon. Once, when Rumi sent his son to Damascus to find Shams, who had journeyed to the city to give the tensions surrounding his unorthodox and intense relationship with Rumi a rest, he told Sultan Walad to look in a particular caravanserai, where he would likely find Shams playing backgammon.

I don't complain about this suffocating world.
I am joyful—even when the whole world mourns.
You take pawns from me, but you do not take the king.
I am happy with just the face of the king—
*   may a thousand pawns be taken!*

These games were not just ready metaphors but popular forms of recreation in their daily lives at the time. Shams and Rumi's son 'Ala al-Din both loved playing chess. Rumi's poetry shows how our inner world is a contest for control, just as life in the outer world is a constant struggle for those vying for supremacy and domination. Rumi says that to counter the devastating menace of the desire for supremacy, we should aim to become nothing instead.

DESIRE FOR SUPREMACY

I would need to start another book if I were to relate
the roots and branches of the desire for supremacy.

It's the disobedient horse that Arabs call Satan,
not the herd remaining in the pasture.

Devilry literally means defiance—
a characteristic that deserves to be cursed.

One hundred eaters may fit around the dining spread,
but two eager for supremacy don't fit in the whole world.

Each of them wishes for the other not to exist,
just as a prince kills his father to claim the throne.

Have you heard the saying: "The kingdom is infertile,"
when a contender for kingship does away
with his own relatives out of fear?

The devilish desire for domination is infertile
 and produces no child,
like fire without affinity for anyone.

The devil burns and rips apart whatever he finds,
and devours himself if he finds nothing else.

So become nothing and save yourself from his teeth.
He has a heart hard as an anvil—
don't seek mercy from it.

Fear not the anvil when you become nothing.
Learn every day a lesson from your absolute poverty instead.

*   *   *

In the existence of your love,
I have become so nonexistent
that nonexistence is better
than a thousand existences.

Every morning of my retreat, I was responsible for making breakfast for Baba. Since I'd starved myself for most of my life, I hadn't a clue how to cook. But I was in luck, since a typical Turkish breakfast usually consists of boiled eggs, cheese, cucumbers, tomatoes, honey, bread, yogurt, and tea. Baba taught me how to boil eggs in the tin vessel traditionally used for brewing Turkish coffee.

After a week of preparing the usual breakfast fare, I decided to get creative and cook Baba an omelet. But when I placed the sizzling tomato, onion, and cheese omelet in front of him, he acted like nothing was different. Perhaps because he sensed my ego was hungering for a compliment, he didn't dispatch one. He just proceeded to eat the omelet as if nothing had changed. Maybe serving an omelet wasn't culturally sensitive, I thought, since he'd never asked for one. Either way, I got the message that I should probably go back to boiling his eggs in the Turkish coffee tin.

The evening after I had served my omelet, Baba let us know that he would make dinner that night—reversing the usual routine of the students serving the teacher. Though I offered to help, Baba would not let me in the kitchen while he cooked, so I took my seat at the table and waited with anticipation to find out what traditional Turkish fare he'd prepared. While I knew Baba had many things to teach me—Turkish cuisine wasn't what I had been expecting.

When Baba entered the room with a large sizzling pot, he made sure to place it right in front of me first. As he removed the lid, he unveiled a giant sizzling egg frittata, unlike any I had ever seen. Sliding a steaming slice onto my plate first, his eyes seemed to say, "Now, that's an omelet." Unable to contain his enormous grin as we dined on his creation, it was clear he had had the last laugh.

CARAVAN FROM EGYPT

The sugary lips of a sweetheart brought news:
"A caravan from Egypt has arrived!"

A hundred camels—all sugar and candy!
O Lord, what a fine gift!

"A candle has arrived at midnight!
A soul has entered the heart of a corpse!"

I said: "Speak plainly!"
She said: "You-know-who has arrived."

My heart flew up in joy,
and placed a ladder on intellect's edge.

It ran to the roof for the sake of love,
seeking a sign of this good news.

Suddenly, it saw from the rooftop
a world outside our world—
an all-encompassing ocean in a jug,
a sky in the form of dust.

On the roof sat a king,
wearing the clothes of a watchman—
an infinite garden and paradise
in that gardener's chest.

His image traveled from breast to breast,
sharing words from the king of the heart.

O image of that fine king,
escape not from my eyes!
Refresh my heart for a moment!

Shams of Tabriz has seen no-place—
and from no-place he built a place.

THE STRUGGLE AGAINST
THE SELF

◆

The struggle against the ego is more challenging than any war fought on the battlefield. The Prophet Muhammad said that the jihad, or struggle, against the self was the greatest struggle of all: it is the most difficult and most important battle of our lives. Rumi similarly saw the greatest enemy as the base or animal self. For Rumi, our lower self is the mother of all idols—worse than the hatred and deceit of any enemy. Rumi incorporates many images of war to capture how intense the struggle is to conquer and annihilate the self.

From the heart to the beloved, there is a path, a path!
and one who does not know this is forgiven, forgiven!
Every day in this spiritual circle, there is a battle, a battle.
You think that this is exaggeration, exaggeration!

Through the love and guidance of a shaykh, a dervish progresses through different levels of the self. At the beginning of the path, a dervish is ruled by the commanding self, ill with its material and sensual desires and love of itself above all else, including the divine. Then the dervish turns toward remembrance of the beloved and in asking for repentance and forgiveness when doing wrong, the blaming self emerges. If a dervish progresses further on the path, she will experience the inspired self (which seeks after love and good deeds), the secure self (rooted in complete trust in the beloved and a constant state of remembrance), the contented self (which accepts, with gratitude, whatever the beloved decrees), the gratified self (which is in complete awe of the majesty of the divine), and the complete self (which has replaced selfhood with love of the divine and transformed into the light of mystic knowledge).

YOUR LIPS

Don't pollute your lips by kissing every mouth
  and delicious dish—
better they become drunk and sweet
from the beloved's lips.

Then the odor of others' lips won't corrupt yours,
and your love will become immaterial—
pure and one.

Those lips that kiss the donkey's ass—
how should the Messiah bless those lips
with his sugar kiss?

Know that everything other than
the ancient light is contingent.
Why do you sit on a heap of dung and expect a spectacle?

When the compost has been annihilated
in the heart
of a vegetable garden,
it's delivered from dinginess and adds flavor to food.

As long as you're impure, how will you taste
the pleasure of veneration?
Go beyond your conditioning to the blessed and transcendent!

The Messiah came as the remedy for the whole world,
by the command of the same hand
that held all the hands prohibited from the sour stew.

When Moses washed his hands and lips of Pharaoh's favors,
the ocean of generosity gave him the white hand of light.

If you want to save the stomach and lips from all impurities,
be full of pearls but bitter on the surface,
like the ocean.

Be careful! Cast your glance away from others,
for that eye is jealous.
Be careful! Keep your stomach empty,
for he has set a table for you.

If a dog becomes full, it will not catch any hunting game,
for the racing and running of aspiration
come from hunger's fire.

Where are a pure hand and pure lips to receive a pure cup?
Where is a spry Sufi to fetch the halva?

Embody the truth in these words,
O you from him, who passes the wine and cup among us!

Rumi calls the mystic path the way of the battlefield. Rumi frequently paints the self as lying in wait—ready to pounce in ambush. Any progress made on the spiritual path is sitting prey for the self, which tries to steal back a dervish's attention and heart.

> In poverty be poor and in purity pure.
> Enter onto the way of the battlefield with poverty and purity.
> If your enemy boasts he has one hundred swords,
> what wound can he make if he sees nothing—
>   he can only brag.

A dervish must be equipped and armed with the virtues of spiritual poverty and purity when faced with his inner enemies. Foes and detractors may come from within—such as envy, hatred, and greed—or from without in the form of others driven by judgment, jealousy, and ignorance. Despite these threats, a dervish must not fear and must stay steadfast on the mystic path.

> Never do we fear the wounds of arrows and daggers,
> nor do we fear shackles on the feet or blades on the neck.
> Fervently spirited, we are the hell of vampires.
> We're even less fearful of what people say and don't.

Rumi refers to mystics as martyrs in a holy war—the war with the self. And the battlefield is love! The self must be martyred for true union with the divine. Mystic holy warriors slay hypocrisy and separation from the divine with their sword of truth. It is in the death of the self that the dervish finds everlasting life. The mystic is a master in the combat of annihilation against the self and the worldly mode of being.

WE ARE SUFIS

We are Sufis, and we threw off our cloaks.
We don't wish to regain what we've already lost.
For our loss, we've already been recompensed by God,
so no worldly compensation will do—
we're cleansed now of greed, intention, and need.

Out of the salty and fatal waters we've emerged,
and headed toward Kawthar,
the heavenly spring,
to approach pure wine.

O world! For all you did to others—
the unfaithfulness, artful tricks,
and playing so hard to get—
we'll torment you with the same in retaliation,
for we're martyrs in this war.

Just so you know: the servants of God the Pure
are fierce and combative.

They'll uproot the worldly manner of hypocrisy,
and pitch their tents atop of the rampart
of the world in victory.

These martyrs have become warriors again—
these captives of worldly life have achieved victory again!

They have arisen from nonexistence,
calling upon those still bound to earthly life:
"See us, if you are not blind,

so you may know there's an abundance
of suns in nothingness,
and what is a sun here
is just a faint star there
in nonexistence."

The people bound to their corporeal life reply:
"O brother, how can existence be found in nonexistence?
How is it possible for a thing to be present
in its contrary state?"

Just as he brings forth the living from the dead,
nonexistence is the hope of genuine worshippers.

Is not the farmer whose barn is empty,
happy and joyful in his hope
for what is now nothing?

He is so, since what he hopes for
grows out of nothingness.
You must grasp this if you are aware of reality.

The dervish is on a quest for a mystical death—this could be one momentous spiritual death of the self, a series of spiritual deaths, or a moment-to-moment death with each breath. Rumi also talks about beheading anger with the sword of patience and being martyred with the sword of nonexistence.

The way I am content with nonexistence—
why so much advice about existence?
The day they kill me with that sword of nonexistence—
who will cry for me? I will laugh at whoever does!

Both Rumi and Shams wrote many poems about the mystical shedding of the blood of the lover. Rumi asks: How can you find rest and peace in this world? Let love flay you alive so that not an ounce of selfhood remains and you can finally truly live.

> *In the army of love, when they spill blood,*
> *they sharpen their swords with pieces of me.*
> *I am drowning in my ocean–like chest.*
> *Tell my friends to keep away!*

Of course, the blood that is shed is a libation for the sweet lips of the beloved. Eventually, the battlefield of love is given up for the banquet table of love. Instead of fighting the self, the dervish begins feasting on her nonexistence—subsisting only on the nourishing blessings of the beloved. In the words of Rumi: "What is the means of ascension to heaven? This not-being. Not-being is the creed and religion of the lovers."

> *Because of your fortitude, neither friend nor enemy remain.*
> *At your banquet table, neither goblet nor pitcher remain.*
> *O beloved, I assume that you drank my blood too.*
> *Finally, on your lips of honey, my sweet scent remains.*

Sacrifice of the self to the beloved is a noble achievement—but the path does not stop there. It is not just the self that needs to be annihilated: a dervish must also sever all his inner attachments to the world and life itself to be fully subsisting in the presence of divine love.

> *Those who have happened upon the lane of the gnostics,*
> *are alert and happy until the trumpet blasts.*
> *One tribe has surrendered to self-sacrifice,*
> *while the other is free from self, life, and the world.*

Subsistence in the divine is the final goal for an annihilated self. Though Rumi himself was Sunni, he became familiar with the rituals and community of Shia Muslims in Aleppo while living in Syria. In his poetry, he mentions Imam Ali, the son-in-law and cousin of the Prophet Muhammad, whose descendants Shia Muslims see as the rightful heirs to Muslim leadership. All hearts, Rumi suggests, no matter how brilliant, courageous, or blessed, should seek refuge completely in God—the source of all.

THE LION OF GOD

The Prophet told Ali:
"Ali, you are the brave and heroic lion of God the Truth."

But don't be so confident about your being like a lion,
and seek sanctuary in the shade of the truth.

Seek refuge in the shade of that Intellectual Being,
which no unwarranted, reputed saying or quotation
could mislead you from.

Rumi praises dervishes in his poetry as courageous warriors, treading a difficult and narrow path back to the divine. The path is lined with dangers of many kinds. Dervishes who have tamed their worst instincts—their anger, their need for attention, their preoccupation with reputation—have little to fear. For those mystics, the dangers will bow down or pass by them on the road.

We are real men, dwelling in a narrow valley.
We are such that wolves and lions pass by us.
With poverty and purity we have mingled,
like ewes and lambs at suckling-time.

In the wake of a mystic death, the heart whirls without interruption and the battlefield is cleared. There is no longer any war against the self: struggle has been replaced with union and a mystical wedding with the divine. The mystic banquet table is set.

> *Today: circumambulation, circumambulation,*
>   *circumambulation!*
> *The crazy one is forgiven, forgiven, forgiven!*
> *No war—or battlefields, battlefields, battlefields!*
> *Just union and marriage, marriage, marriage!*

In the end, annihilation is abandoned in favor of subsistence in the divine. No longer weighed down by the battle against the self, a dervish can partake fully in the feast of mystical communion.

DYING IN LOVE

> *Now die, die, in this love, die!*
> *When you've died in this love,*
> *you'll all receive a new spirit!*

> *Go die, die, and from this death, don't fear—*
> *for from this dust you'll rise*
> *and seize the heavens.*

> *Die, die, and break free from this self,*
> *for this self is like a chain,*
> *and you are its prisoner.*

Grab an axe to dig free from this prison—
when you've broken the prison,
you'll all be kings and princes.

Die, die in the presence of the beautiful king!
When you've died before the king,
you'll all be kings and celebrated!

Die, die, and emerge from this cloud.
When you emerge from this cloud,
you'll all be illuminating full moons.

You are silent, you are silent—
for silence is the breath of death.
So don't fret—since even in death,
there is life and breath.

* * *

In everyone's hands, you can find scraps of goodness.
The quarry of grace and the mine of beauty are my desire!
The bread and water served by the wheel of heaven
are fortunes flowing like a volatile torrent.
But I am a fish, a whale—
and swimming in the Sea of Oman
is my only desire.

Gradually, without me realizing it, I was becoming free from the negativity that had sent me to the madhouse. Living in such a close-knit community—which itself resembled a madhouse—I didn't have much time for restless rumination and feelings of alienation. An early Sufi woman, Umm Abdullah, once said, "Being in the company of one's spiritual brethren in this world is the consolation for being in the abode of materiality."

My dervish brothers took care of my every need: anytime I asked for something, from dry cleaning to *sahlep*—a heated cinnamon milk drink—it magically appeared in an instant. The dervishes seized every moment as an opportunity to compete lovingly in service, understanding that salvation from the ego is only really purchased with servitude.

"Without love and friendship, you see, it's not possible to progress on the path," Baba said to me. This is why he was so insistent on me spending as much time as possible with his dervish disciples—to learn how to practice friendship, be in community, and accept the support and love of selfless mystics on the path. Being absorbed in a dynamic communal life was an ongoing lesson in mutual care, compassion, and love.

Even though I was the only woman embedded in our Sufi fraternity, I did not feel any different from my dervish brothers, since they always went out of their way to be respectful and gracious—which was in keeping with the Mevlevi Order's long tradition of including women. Rumi had female disciples of his own, as did his son. In Rumi's time and even centuries before, there were female dervishes and masters. In addition, many wealthy women offered charity to receive Sufi blessings and established endowments to support Sufi communities.

Rumi even performed *sema* with female singers and musicians, which was scandalous at the time—and in most places still is. He also attended women-only *sema* sessions. Rumi was friends with women of low stature—like tavern dancers—and high status, including the most powerful woman in the Seljuk state, a Christian queen from Georgia who was married to a sultan and became Rumi's disciple. Rumi reportedly showed gentleness and respect to his wives.

It was Baba who set the tone for mutual appreciation and respect. I never felt unsafe or unwelcome among my dervish brothers. Baba's rigorous enforcement of proper conduct, mindfulness, and service helped us relate to one another not through fixed categories like gender or nationality, but through intentional acts of service and friendship. We were not men or women—we were servants of love and compassion, broken human hearts striving to become whole. Without the constant support of my openhearted dervish brothers, I knew I would never finish my forty-day retreat.

SPIRITUAL FRIENDSHIP

◆

Whereas the West uses the term "saint" for a pious soul devoted to purifying the heart and performing selfless acts, Sufis use the term "friend" as in "the friends of God." Rumi refers to mystics in his poetry often as "friends." Rumi also refers to the divine as the "friend." As the Qur'an says, "Truly for the friends of God, there is no fear nor shall they grieve." Trusting fully in the divine, the Sufi has no reason to feel anxious or sad.

Be a friend, so you may find countless friends—
for without friends, you will be left helpless.

There is no greater friend for the mystic than the divine. The divine is the ultimate friend—the best provider, the ideal consoler, and the original source of unconditional love. However, a Sufi must also have friendship with other mystics on the path to flourish. As Rumi advises: "Be a friend, so that you may find innumerable friends—for without friends you'll be left helpless."

Dervishes focus on nurturing godly friendship between mystic hearts. Rumi wrote that the best way to taste paradise was to speak well of others. Friendship was best forged by doing good acts of service for others. As Shams explains, "The purpose of life is for two friends to meet each other and to sit together face-to-face in the spirit of God, far from earthly desires.

The goal is not bread or the baker, not the butcher shop or the butcher. It's simply this very hour, while I'm sitting here at ease in your company."

If you sit with ignorant people, you'll turn cold.
But if you dwell with enlightened souls,
  you'll be a true human being.
Now go and build a hermit cell like gold inside a furnace.
But if you go out from the furnace, you'll freeze.

Rumi recommended avoiding the company of common people and fools. Instead, he advised seeking out the virtuous. In his own life, however, he did not only surround himself with pious and morally upstanding people. On the contrary, he intentionally befriended "bad" people to help guide them to be and do good.

LOVE'S FRIEND

What is it like to befriend love?
Nothing except to separate from the heart's desire.
To become blood—to swallow one's own blood,
and lie at loyalty's door with the dogs.

Love's friend is a devotee.
For him, there is no difference
between death, departing, and being.

On the way, Muslims, be shielded by peace
and strive for devotion,
for these martyrs haven't patience with death—
they love annihilation.

Flee, if you want, from suffering and fate—
but their fear is to be without suffering.
Go be the pretentious believer who fasts on Ashura—
for you aren't made to battle in Karbala that day.

Spiritual companionship was one of the most important as-
pects of mystic life in early Sufism. Many felt that nothing was
more beneficial than being immersed in a mystic community.
Some even dared to go so far as to say that commitment to one's
spiritual companions was more beneficial and desirable than
being with one's own family; this belief eventually died out as
stronger currents encouraging family life and a permanent res-
idence prevailed.

If you socialize with anyone with whom your heart
*   doesn't feel whole,*
and the anxiety of your bodily concerns isn't driven away—
take care and avoid his company.
Otherwise, the souls of the dear ones won't pardon you!

Medieval dervish manuals warned Sufis to avoid associat-
ing with non-Sufis and cautioned them against revealing secret
doctrines to non-Sufis or accepting any presents or charity from
them. Thus, while medieval dervishes were known for being
incredibly generous and giving charity, they socialized mostly
among themselves. As Shams said, "The first effect on someone
who finds his way to our gatherings is that he will chill; he'll lose
interest in the conversations of others. He may not only become
cool to their conversations; he cannot even join them." A dervish
is spiritually transformed in the community of his mystical com-
panions: just being in their presence is healing and soul changing.

O enamored one, grab the hem of the lover's robe.
Fruit itself is made to hang from the tree.
A Byzantine goes toward a Byzantine,
and a Zanzibari toward a Zanzibari.
A grape always takes its color from other grapes.

Medieval manuals also cautioned dervishes against fraternizing with those who assume the guise of knowledge by being Sufis only in name and appearance. They warn against associating with experts in the religious sciences whose desire for power and praise could pollute the purity of the Sufis and the spiritual harmony of dervish communities. There was also the risk that those who pride themselves on religious knowledge would be envious of the devotion and piety of the Sufis.

THE SOUL'S KERNEL

When you see devoted souls benefiting,
you'll feel envious like the devil would too.

Just like an unstable person who
doesn't want anyone else to be stable.

To save yourself this devilish grudge,
pivot from pretention to faithfulness.

But if there's no devotion in you,
you'd better stay silent—
since speech is structured
to proclaim the self:
"I" and "We."

Speech unspoken in the heart is the gain of the mind—
in silence, the soul's kernel grows a hundred times larger.

You spend from the mind
for thoughts to be translated into words.
Spend less to keep your mind precious.

The contemplative who speaks little
has a range of thoughts—
as the layers of talking expand,
the kernel of the mind shrinks.

Look at the kernels of these three
when they've passed beyond immaturity:
the walnut, the almond, and the pistachio.

Whoever disobeys the divine rule becomes a devil,
envying the fortune of the righteous.

If you are devoted to your covenant with God,
he'll kindly keep his covenant with you.

But you turn a blind eye on your covenant with God,
and do not listen to his saying:
"Remember me, and I will remember you."

Listen to God the beloved when he summons you:
"Fulfill your covenant, and I will fulfill mine."

Rumi warns against sharing mystical experiences or truths with those who are not close dervish friends. Spiritual knowledge is not for those who have not been privy to it. Those who are not mystically inclined are not capable of receiving accounts of spiritual experiences and comprehending mystical insights.

> *Don't tell secrets to those who aren't confidants,*
> *or stories of the friend to those who've been rebuffed.*
> *Don't speak to outsiders except about outside things.*
> *Don't say anything to a thorn-eating camel*
>   *except about thorns!*

According to Rumi, a mystic must realize that she should no longer associate with those who do not help nurture her spiritual development. Those who are not supporting the mystic on the spiritual path are like deadweight: they keep the mystic from ascending to truth and drawing nearer to love. In order to soar, the mystic must let them go.

> *It was enough for me—enough for me—and I put an end to it.*
> *I've turned my back to lousy friends.*
> *I'm praying again in your direction.*
> *I have sacrificed all the carrion to the vulture.*

Rumi compels us to question: What or who is the carrion in our life? What or who do we need to sacrifice to find peace? Is it toxic friends? A relationship? Or aspects of the self—the carnage of our own delusions, anxieties, and ambitions?

> *Those who cut ties with good friends*
> *fall under the spells and schemes of charlatans.*
> *They limp behind like lame goats,*
> *before wolves tear them apart—bit by bit.*

Rumi uses hunting imagery to describe the dangers of associating with false friends. Those whose hearts are not pure threaten to ambush the people of purity—they watch their every move until they see an opportunity to strike.

> *Those tracking you night and day,*
> *are like hunters hidden in the bush—quick to attack.*
> *They'll sever you from anyone*
> *   with whom you're harmonious.*
> *If you don't go along, they'll take you and drag you away.*

Rumi also critiques those who hunt for others to praise them—who make friends just to feed their egos. He criticizes the eagerness some have to gain others' attention as they hunt for transitory friends out of their delusions of grandeur and insatiable need to be recognized and adored.

YOUR TRAP

> *O brother! You've made many friends*
> *   by winning people's hearts,*
> *but then abandoned them afterward.*

> *Since you were born, it's been your business to hunt people,*
> *entrapping them by friendship.*

> *Go delve into your chases, crowds, vanity, and egoic being,*
> *and see if you can find anything stable and worthwhile.*

> *The majority of your life has passed,*
> *   and your days are numbered—*
> *yet you're still busy hunting for people's attention.*

You grab one and release another from your snare—
and then, like other dishonorable folks,
you hunt for another!

This one too, you'll leave behind,
  as you start seeking another—
as if you're just playing like an immature child.

Night arrives and you have no catch left in your trap,
which has brought you nothing but trouble and limitations.

You see: you've been entrapping yourself the whole time,
and that's why you're like a captive—
disappointed by desire,
and deprived of satisfaction.

Rumi's son Sultan Walad did not believe in preaching about Sufism from the pulpit. Even when asked by a Seljuk prince to do so, he initially said no. He explained, "I have already said what can be said here. The rest of our words are not those kinds of words that can be told from pulpits. People's minds cannot reach the delicacies of these truths. These meanings ruin their mental abilities." Sultan Walad believed in spiritual elitism: for him, the divine secrets were only sent to the spiritually "elect." As he explains:

How can you deliver a secret belonging to the high to the low? Can a bird that has fallen into a trap fly? Can an old woman fight like a brave champion? Those who are veiled from God cannot reach the station of possessing spiritual states and words. Those mystical states and words belong to the King. Who can be privy to that secret by struggling and striving for his lower soul? Food meant for a falcon will cause a small bird to suffocate and choke. One should accept little as much. One should be content with a pitcher rather than the sea.[8]

Sultan Walad revered the mystic knowledge of Persian philosophers like Ibn Sina (d. 1037), and believed that the "common herd of men" was not capable of grasping such deep mystical and philosophical matters. While such a view may sound harsh and judgmental, this was not an insight that was particular to Sufism and it had its roots in the ancient world. In fact, for Sufis, keeping mystic secrets among the spiritually elite is considered an act of compassion: one should not reveal things to people that they cannot comprehend.

Rumi wrote a litany of sorts for those who suffer envy that they may be endowed instead with patience and redemption. It makes sense that dervishes were targets of envy, as they sacrificed each moment of their lives to trying to become a perfected human being in compassion, ethical conduct, and devotion to the divine. To those who are ruled by their base selves, the people of purity are an affront, as their polished hearts mirror back to those governed by their animal nature what they are and what they are not.

PRAYER FOR PROTECTION FROM ENVY

O you, provider of nourishment, constancy, and stability—
may you deliver the people from instability.

May you make wayward souls upright,
to cope with demands requiring stability.

May you bestow patience upon them,
and let the righteous side of their scale
weigh more heavily than the evil.

And may you deliver them from the tricks
and crafts of visual artists.

O generous one, redeem them from their envying,
so they aren't cursed like the devil from envy.

Oh, how the whole world burns with envy
for the fleeting happiness of wealth,
and the passing pleasures of the body.

Look at kings who wage war against their relatives,
and kill them out of envy.

Or lovers of the same floozy
out for each other's blood,
who take aim at one another's life.

Read the stories of Vis and Ramin or Khosraw and Shirin
to learn what those fools did out of envy.

The lover and the beloved both perished,
while their passion was just as paltry
as nothingness and their nonexistent being.

God is so pure he can bring nonexistences together,
and makes nonexistence fall
in love with nonexistence.

Then, in those hearts that are untrue hearts,
envy arises and the nonexistent state
gets disturbed by the existence of envy.

* * *

Be melting snow—
wash yourself of yourself.

Toward the end of my retreat, I was surprised by the appearance at Baba's apartment of a beautiful young woman who wept uncontrollably from the first moment of her arrival from Syria. During a monthlong retreat at the shrine of Sayyida Zainab, the granddaughter of the Prophet Muhammad, she had received a spiritual sign to travel to Istanbul. Her constant crying reminded me of Ghufayra al-Abida, an early Sufi woman who became blind from devotional weeping. When someone said to her, "How devastating is blindness!" she replied, "No, being veiled from God is worse."

"Zemzem, you will teach Samira how to turn; this will be your service," Baba said. I tried to discern the cause of her constant weeping through intuition and simple questions, but she was unable to speak. She was drowning in a flood of her own tears.

Eventually, I gleaned that although she had had a very successful career back home in North America, her family's roots were in Pakistan and she was feeling pulled by the divine to the mystic path. She seemed to be stuck and straddling two worlds—the soul-crushing grind of ambition and material success and the overpowering spiritual realm of the divine. Since words couldn't really reach her, I hoped maybe movement would.

I put the whirling board down and began to pour the mystic knowledge that Baba had entrusted to my heart into hers. When she stepped onto the board and began to turn counterclockwise around her heart, a playful smile—instead of tears—slipped across her lips and a blinding beam of sunlight suddenly flooded the room through the stained-glass windows.

GO, FRIENDS

Go, comrades, and fetch our beloved friend!
Bring to me at last that elusive idol!

With sweet songs and golden excuses,
haul home the beautiful-faced good moon.

And if he promises: "I will come another time,"
every promise is a trick—he will cheat you!

His breath is so warm that with magic and enchantments,
he can tie water in a knot and turn air solid.

With blessedness and happiness,
when my ideal one appears,
sit back and behold the miracles of God.

When his majesty shines
the glory of the beautiful is gone,
For his sun-like face extinguishes the lamps.

Go, O easygoing heart, to Yemen, to my soulmate.
Give my greetings and my service
to that priceless gemstone.

SPIRITUAL POVERTY

◆

Rumi was not interested in the comforts of an expensive meal or the general security of wealth—he was focused almost exclusively on crossing the bridge to the beloved. Rumi turned his gaze away from the bustling life of the bazaar to the spiritual fruits and blessings of the hidden realm of the heart. Weary and suspicious of life in the world of the living, he devoted himself to running away from his own existence and fixated instead on the eternal presence. While he did offer guidance to Seljuk sultans, queens, and diplomats, Rumi did not let his proximity to power and influence tempt his gaze away from the divine to the glittering charms of the world.

> *Poverty is the essence, and all except poverty is transient.*
> *Poverty is healing, and all except poverty is illness.*
> *The whole world is vanity and deceit,*
> *and poverty is the treasure and purpose of the world.*

In Rumi's time, spiritual poverty was celebrated as a virtue. Medieval dervish manuals celebrated the merits of a total renunciatory life in which the Sufi abandoned work for profit in favor of laboring for divine love. In fact, revered theologian al-Ghazali dedicated an entire section to "Poverty and Abstinence" in his celebrated book *The Revival of the Religious Sciences*. He traces these two virtues back to the Prophet Muhammad, who instructed his followers to love the poor and framed this love as a key to paradise. The Prophet's exalted humility was for Rumi, like Muslims today, a model for a life of spiritual poverty—that is, a life not defined by attachment to the material world and its comforts and charms.

> I'm happy without silver and silk.
> In suffering, I'm tranquil and I'm joyful in fear.
> With the wine of surrender, I'm happy for all eternity.
> Don't assume I'm half-happy like you.

As a respected teacher, jurist, and theologian, Rumi was well aware of the ego traps of wealth, high status, and prestigious positions. He criticized the greed, boasting, and anxiety of the rich and powerful. Since fortunes come and go, he warned of the dangers of being attached to the wheel of fortune, whose fickleness could suddenly destroy a life.

> If the wheel of fortune continues to serve you—
> don't accept it, for it will degrade you in the end.
> Unexpectedly, after making you drunk with a drink,
> it will place its hand upon the neck of another beloved.

Spiritual poverty means one is empty of envy, greed, pride, jealousy, arrogance, and ostentation. Instead of worshipping the self and competing with others in wealth, attention, and recognition, a Sufi strives to awaken to divine love. What is wealth in this world when compared with the divine hidden mysteries? Of course, when a mystic heart becomes poor, or emptied of the world, all that remains is the radiance of the divine essence.

My friend, you ask me for my heart and gold.
The truth is, I have neither one to give.
Gold? What gold does a poor man have?
Since when does a lover have a heart left to give?

For Rumi, the mystic path is for the unconventional, the nonconformists, and the rule breakers. The mystic way is not for the wealthy—addicted as they are to greed and far removed from the rich spiritual truths hidden behind the veil.

Anyone who's employed is not one of the friends,
for our profession is the profession of the unemployed.
This is the road of highway robbers and roving knights.
How could it be a place for the rich and those with gold?

One who is keeping busy in the realm of materiality is not one of the "friends"—one of the mystics. In this world of striving for wealth and hoarding resources, Rumi forces us to reevaluate our communal values. What "work" do we devote ourselves to in this precious life—the work of a paying job, or the priceless work of becoming an awakened and perfected human being? In whose service are we employed? Are we living to serve a boss and company—or something greater? For Rumi, "there is no job more beautiful than joblessness."

The night has disappeared, and I am still with my wine-seller.
With your good fortune, I am always at my work.
I am also the lover, the lovesick, and the beloved.
I am also the gathering, the nightingale, and the rose garden.

In the presence of love, all divisions collapse; even the lover and beloved can no longer tell themselves apart! In the ecstasy of intimacy, as Rumi shows, there is no separation or distinction. To be empty in our hands and heart is to taste the sweet nectar of liberation.

> *The emptier our hands and hearts are of everything,*
>   *the better—*
> *for freedom of the heart is better than anything "better."*
> *The sweet delight of spiritual poverty for just one moment*
> *is better than the splendor of a hundred thousand Caesars.*

For Rumi, true greatness and everlasting life can only be found by stepping bravely upon the path of poverty. But how will your heart find what it is seeking if it is overburdened with thoughts of work? How will you know the true value of it? What truly will bring your heart rest?

> *I don't have a chosen one other than you—what can I do?*
> *I don't have a remedy for my sad heart—what can I do?*
> *You say: "Until when will we whirl because of fate?"*
> *I don't have another job except this—what can I do?*

Rumi's emphasis on the merits of spiritual poverty brings to mind a related verse from the Qur'an: "O humanity, you are poor and in need of God, and God is the Self-Sufficient and Praiseworthy." In his poetry, Rumi paints the bazaar, or marketplace, as a symbol of the temptations of the material world. For him, the best job of all is not to be found in the bazaar, but in the heart—in chasing after the beloved.

> *Exalted souls endowed with knowledge and wisdom*
> *are always provided with subsistence.*
> *But for those with a mind empty of wisdom—*
> *worries about wealth are in its place.*

Although Rumi was from the Persian elite and a respected
scholar and jurist, many of his followers were laborers and crafts-
men, and he socialized with men and women from different classes
and backgrounds. In addition to religious teachers and Qur'an re-
citers, his circle of disciples and friends included carpenters, doc-
tors, musicians, astrologers, tanners, dancers, and butchers.

> *They've spoken about spiritual poverty*
> *with all kinds of words.*
> *They've pierced the pearl of meaning in ignorance.*
> *But since they never awakened*
> *to the universe's secrets,*
> *they blabbered on and went to sleep.*

Rumi mocks those who pretend to practice spiritual poverty
but understand nothing of its essence or purpose. Their idle talk is
useless in trying to unlock the secrets of the universe and human
heart. Rumi tried to avoid idle talk himself, and in his poetry he
cautions against it. The job of the lover is to sing in praise of his or
her beloved! It is to share the story of how the heart was captured
by the divine. It is to tell the tale of leaving the world behind.

> *The job of the lover is to sing songs!*
> *To mention the idol with no trace!*
> *To tell the story of the snare and the bait!*
> *Or to talk about leaving behind one's home and store.*

What need does the true lover have for the "store"? The
lover must leave the marketplace behind and turn instead to
contemplating and loving the divine with each breath. Instead
of hunting after money, the dervish is engaged in a nonstop
game of snare and bait with the beloved. True love is tasted
when we abandon our conditioning—from society, culture, and
the family—and our desire for wealth and gain.

One sip from your wineglass is completeness, completeness!
Except for love of you, what is in my heart? What?
In my love for you, the heart's blood is halal, halal,
and resting from love is haram, haram!

For Rumi, just tasting the wine of divine essence—the ecstasy of love—is perfection. What is religiously ordained, or *halal*, Rumi maintains, is the sacrifice of the heart—to love. And thus, what is religiously forbidden, or *haram*, is taking a break from being completely absorbed in divine love.

Without you, life is haram, O dearest.
Without you, what life is there for me, O dearest?
I swear that life without you is just death
with the name of life stamped upon it, O dearest.

A life lived without love of the divine, Rumi suggests, breaks Islamic law. Like his father, who was an Islamic cleric, Rumi was an Islamic jurist and issued fatwas, or religious opinions. Thus, he knew Islamic law very well. Both Rumi and Shams were Sunni Muslims. But while Rumi belonged to the Hanafi school of jurisprudence, his teacher, Shams, belonged to the Shafi'i school of jurisprudence. Their adherence to different schools of jurisprudence in the Sunni tradition was not an issue or conflict. However, in his poetry, Rumi boldly points to the lack of "love" discourse in both schools of jurisprudence.

LOVE IS NOTHING

Love is nothing but happiness and loving kindness.
It is nothing but an open heart and guidance.

Abu Hanifa did not teach love.
Shafi'i had no tradition of it.

"Licit" and "illicit" are only viable until the hour of death,
but there's no end to the knowledge of lovers.

Lovers are drowned in sugar-water.
Egypt has no complaint about sugar.

How can the soul of a drunk not utter thanks
for a wine without boundary or end?

Whoever you've seen sorrowful and scowling
   is not a lover,
nor from the province of love.

Otherwise, every bud is a veil of a garden—
envy and jealousy have no contagion.

The beginner on this path of love
is the one who is not aware of beginning.

Become nonexistent from your own self,
because there's no crime worse
than your own self-centered existence.

Never become a shepherd—
be a servant instead.
Shepherding is nothing but a barrier
to spiritual practice and divine care.

God alone suffices for the suffering of many servants,
but the servants are without this sufficiency and knowledge.

He says: "This is problematic and allegorical.
While this is clear, and this is not allegory."

A blind man's foot knocked over a pitcher.
He said: "The doorkeeper is not careful.
What are pitchers and glasses doing in the middle of the path?
The road is not clear of these pots.

Take the pitchers off the path!
The doorkeeper is bad at his job!"

The doorkeeper answered:
"O blind man, there is no pitcher on the path.
You have no knowledge of the path!
You've left the path and are going to the pitcher—
that is a mistake."

Listen, there's no sign on the way of religion
  from beginning to end,
except for your drunkenness.

You are a sign, and a seeker of signs.
There's no better sign than the seeking of a sign itself.

You are astray from the path.
Otherwise, on the path of striving,
no striver is without his wages.

Just as whoever does an atom's weight of good
  shall see a reward,
an atom's weight of evil is not without punishment.

An atom of good is not without an unveiling—
so open your eyes,
if you are not blind.

Every vegetable is a token of water—
what is there that is not a tributary to that?

Enough, this water has enough tokens—
a thirsty soul has no need of guidance.

Despite his own religious legal knowledge and position, Rumi was critical of religious jurists and those fixated on the letter of the law. He was suspicious of the hypocrisy of judges who sought after status and power. Rumi favored praising and pleasing the supreme judge of the universe instead of arguing about the finer points of Islamic jurisprudence on matters such as whether music and whirling were permissible.

Our judge is not like other judges.
His interest is not in fatwas on satin and scissors.
Our judge has been a lover from beginningless time—
with anything else, the judge of love is not happy.

Rumi was less interested in the nuances of adjudicating the practices of daily life according to Islamic law than he was in being a judge of love. Rumi received many complaints and much criticism for his "unorthodox" behavior, such as his incorporation of poetry, whirling, and music into worship, from clerics and even other dervishes. In response to his gatherings, jurists issued fatwas to forbid *sema* and the playing of the rebab.

See the partying of those drunkards in the wheeling heavens.
Be in the melting pot of nonexistence and see the existent ones.
Keep your hands from this world and the next—
    and hold back your feet too!
See in spiritual poverty the majesty of the masters.

Despite these critiques of Rumi's unconventional practices, Rumi did not contest or debate them in public—he just kept on playing music and hosting whirling ceremonies. Thanks to Rumi's exemplary virtue, extensive religious knowledge, and polished heart, he did not suffer the wrath of the jurists who found his untraditional practices innovative and heretical. Whereas judges were fixated on transmitting religious knowledge through speech and debate, Rumi believed that practicing spiritual poverty was the best way to receive spiritual insight.

THE RANK OF SPIRITUAL POVERTY

Speech is the way to learn the sciences,
and practice the way to learn skills.

But if you desire the rank of spiritual poverty,
sociability and conversation can't help you.
Language and manual effort are of no use.

The soul grasps from the soul how to get there—
not from knowledge shared in discourse or books.

When mystical insights are latent in the heart
  of a spiritual traveler,
she is not yet aware of the spiritual mysteries—
until her heart is opened to the divine light,
which happens when God calls upon her saying:
"Didn't we open your heart?
And relieve you from your burden
which weighed so heavily on your back?

We disclosed hidden insights into your heart—
we expanded your heart."

And yet you're still seeking spiritual illumination
outside of yourself!
You're like a churn full of milk—
why are you still seeking milk from others?

Within you is a boundless spring of milk—
why then are you seeking milk in the pail?

You are a pool with a channel flowing into the sea—
so be ashamed of searching for water in the streamlets!
Was not: "Didn't we expand your heart?"
    enough for you to be enlightened—
yet you are begging elsewhere for spiritual illumination.

Look into the enlightened heart inside you,
if you don't want to be subject
    to the divine reproach
when saying: "Can you not see?"

*   *   *

The soul that was an enemy has become a stranger.
The rational man who was a doctor has become a lunatic.
All kings hide treasures in ruins.
Our ruin became a ruin because of treasure.

After falling asleep one late night while on my retreat, I dreamed that I was going on a trip to Konya in Turkey, where Rumi is buried. The travelers accompanying me said they wanted to spend time in Istanbul before venturing to Konya. I, however, was very determined to get to Konya as quickly as possible to see the mausoleum of Rumi, as it had been revealed to my heart that something spectacular would be occurring there very soon—but I wasn't told what that miracle would be.

My fellow travelers were skeptical, but they joined me anyway. For the entire length of the trip, I was plunged into a very deep state of meditation, feeling guided to the tomb of Rumi by a force far greater than I had ever felt. The moment that we reached the courtyard of Rumi's tomb, his entire mausoleum lifted up into the air and began whirling in a blinding column of light. When my travel companions saw this, they fell to their knees and repented for their disbelief and begged God for forgiveness. Waking up from the dream in a deep sweat, I resolved to go to Konya after my retreat ended to visit the tomb of Rumi.

When my retreat finally came to an end, and I could leave the apartment building after a month stuck inside and immersed in dervish life, it felt so strange to finally step back into the world— the bustling street scene I had been watching day and night from on high. I felt like I was seeing Istanbul as if for the first time. Everyone seemed so wrapped up in the material world of the living, very unlike the annihilated souls I had been spending all my time with.

I celebrated the conclusion of my retreat by treating myself to a Turkish bath in an Ottoman hammam that has been in operation for more than three hundred years—to baptize my body and begin anew. Entering the busy tourist district of Sultanahmet was overwhelming—the crowded sidewalks, the loud calls to prayer, and the savory scents of the busy cafés. In the heart of the hammam, the Ionic columns, silver bowls, and draped towels made me feel like I had wandered onto the stage of an Isadora Duncan performance.

Through the hazy steam, as Turkish and European women

baked naked on the hot stone in the center, I took one of the silver bowls in my hand and poured water from the two faucets—one hot, one cold—all over my body. I'd forgotten what it felt like to feel my body—having been wrapped up like a mummy in layers of cloth and a headscarf with male dervishes for a month.

As I lay down on the hot, gray stone center, a plump Turkish masseuse with frizzy brown hair scrubbed me roughly with a coarse loofah, scraping away my sins of the past and opening my pores to the cleansing steam of the present.

Looking up at the stars cut in the medieval stone dome, I began to daydream about my next adventure. But my Silk Road fantasy ended before it really even began—when the masseuse threw buckets of water on my soaped-up body from all directions, in what felt like a bizarre hazing ritual. With a lifelong aversion to water in my face, I tried not to panic.

"I am like a baby," I said in elementary Turkish, as I rubbed the soapy bubbles from my eyes.

After I dried off, I stopped in a café for *sahlep*, my beloved winter concoction of warm milk and cinnamon, which I spruced up with a shot of espresso and hot chocolate. It felt so indulgent and luxurious in the wake of my dervish retreat.

On the walk back to Baba's, I wandered through a deserted Ottoman cemetery, weaving through the tall gravestones topped with stone hats to represent the station or profession of each deceased soul—a royal official here, a Sufi shaykh there.

I had never thought about my gravestone before, but looking at the stone Sufi hats adorning the tombs of the dervishes, I was sold. How though, I wondered, could I ship one of these large dervish-hat-topped tombstones to America?

When I returned to Baba's place that evening, I asked how I might get such a tombstone made and brought back to America.

The other dervishes, who were not as accustomed as I was to contemplating and sharing the details of their funeral plans, shook their heads with slight disapproval at me speaking so openly about my final arrangements.

"I have a better idea," Baba said. "When you feel like you're dying, fly to Istanbul and die here—it'll be much cheaper than shipping one to America."

That night, Baba told me he wanted me to commit myself to studying Persian, so that I could read Rumi in the original. While I had studied Persian at Brown, I knew that I would need full immersion if I had any hope of becoming more fluent. But considering the state of affairs between Iran and America, I had little hope of studying Persian in Iran.

Before I left for Turkey, I had applied for an American Center of Iranian Studies fellowship to study Persian and Tajik intensively in Tajikistan. Tajikistan was my best shot at Persian immersion. Since I also spoke Russian (being of Slavic descent), I felt I was in a good position to win the fellowship, but I wasn't counting on it. Baba told me I had no reason to worry, and that my service going forward would be to master Persian to share the real Rumi with the West.

WHO IS IT?

He said: "Who is at the door?"
I said: "Your humble servant."

He said: "What job do you have?"
I said, "Lord, to greet you."

He said: "For how long will you drive?"
I said: "For as long as you say."

He said: "For how long will you boil?"
I said: "Until Resurrection Day."

I laid claim to love.
I swore oaths for the sake of love.
I lost kingship and courage.

He said: "For a claim, the judge needs a witness."
I said: "My tears are my witness,
and the pallor of my face my statement."

He said: "Your witness is null and void—
    your eye is unchaste."
I said: "By the splendor of your justice,
they are just and without atonement."

He said: "Who was your fellow companion?"
I said: "Visions of you, O king!"
He said: "Who summoned you here?"
I said: "The scent of your wine goblet."

He said: "What intention do you have?"
I said: "Faithfulness and friendship."
He said: "What do you want from me?"
I said: "Your all-encompassing grace."

He said: "Where is a more agreeable place?"
I said: "The palace of Caesar."
He said: "What did you see there?"
I said: "A hundred miraculous acts of generosity."

He said: "Why then is it empty?"
I said: "For fear of the highwayman."

He said: "Who is the highwayman?"
I said: "This blame."

He said: "Where is security?"
I said: "In devotion and piety."
He said: "What is devotion?"
I said: "The way of peace."

He said: "Where is calamity?"
I said: "In the street of your love."
He said: "In what condition are you there?"
I said: "A state of perseverance."

I better be silent! For if I were to utter his subtleties,
you would come out of yourself—
and neither door nor roof would remain
in place for you.

THE PATH OF SELF-BLAME

◆

The trophies of this world mean nothing to the mystic lover; the only true goal and reward is experiencing the divine and drawing nearer to the beloved. A mystic is not interested in this world or even paradise; she just longs to be one of the hearts seeking the face and favor of the beloved. A mystic does not seek status, wealth, or a high position. And even if she has attained a high rank, she resists pride and arrogance. Her aim is not to elevate herself but to humble herself.

> *I am not a man of distinction in the village—I'm a buffoon!*
> *I am not the master of the inn—I'm a hooligan!*
> *No, no! I am like a brush in the hand of the painter—*
> *I myself don't even know where I am.*

At a higher level, a mystic can practice the path of self-blame. In this practice, referred to as the Malamatiya tradition, a mystic might pretend to be offensive, ignorant, or blasphemous to invite scorn, derision, and criticism. Inviting negative and damaging attention helps to make his ego less attached to approval and praise. To bait mockery and smash his reputation, a mystic may engage in impolite and even heretical behaviors. Feigning improper behavior also averts the envy of the evil eye from those who are jealous of mystics perceived as especially pious.

One day a rude man said to a dervish:
"You are unknown to anyone here."
The dervish replied: "If common people don't know me,
I know very well who I am."

To invite reproach, a mystic might appear to miss prayers, drink wine, blaspheme the religion, wear fancy clothing, or act insane. Medieval mystics on the path of self-blame would usually avoid public *sema* gatherings, not because they rejected whirling on jurisprudential grounds, but because they were afraid to reveal the true and pure nature of their inner spiritual states.

Love and reputation, O brother, are not compatible.
Don't stand at the door of reputation, O lover.

While on the outside mystics on the path of self-blame may appear to be tricksters, rascals, or rogues, inwardly they always keep a pure state. Instead of building themselves up, they spend their time tearing themselves down. They strip themselves of all forms and become wholly spirit. Dervishes, after all, have a reputation as the wise fools of God—saints posing as rogues to break their own attachment to piety, virtue, and reputation to subsist only in love.

O leaping heart, bound onto the path of blame!
Every moment, wound yourself more than you can bear!
Every instant, ignite fire in a soul!
And in every breath, breathe the breath of ease.

A mystic on the path of self-blame tries to bring blame upon herself from others. This does not mean one finds fault with the self or blames the self for one's suffering. Instead of seeking praise, she seeks derision to help her avoid the ego trappings of admiration and the arrogance of self-worship. The practice of self-blame is no longer really practiced as it was in the past, though a high-level Sufi adept may attempt it with the permission of her shaykh.

Rumi encountered such mystics from a young age in his family's Silk Road journeys, and Shams of Tabriz was also a practitioner of the path of self-blame. On their journey west, Rumi's family visited Nishapur, now in the Islamic Republic of Iran, with its celebrated poets and Malamati mystics who followed the "path of blame." Upon Shams's suggestion and under his protection, Rumi himself practiced acts that would bring gossip and disdain, such as carrying alcohol through the streets of Konya.

I want the wine made of grape syrup.
I want the jolly, drunken mate.

I can detect a scent coming from Hallaj.
So now I want a triumphant drink!

Rumi, like many Persian and Arab poets of the past and present, was drawn to the figure of Mansur al-Hallaj, a controversial mystic and poet who was brutally executed in 922 in Baghdad for reportedly uttering, "I am the Truth," while in a state of ecstatic union with the divine. In Arabic, the words that al-Hallaj said were: *Ana al-haqq.* Al-Haqq, or "The Truth," is one of the ninety-nine names of God in Islam. Al-Hallaj's assertion that he had annihilated his ego and fully merged with the divine was deemed heretical by the authorities, and thus he was put to death.

Mansur al-Hallaj, who said: "I am the Truth,"
swept the dust from every road with the tips of his eyelashes.
He dove into the sea of his own nonbeing.
Then, after that, he pierced the pearl of "I am the Truth."

For centuries and to the present day, Muslims have debated al-Hallaj's words. Are his words a sign of the ultimate submission or a prideful proclamation of presumption? Are they a mark of wisdom or blasphemy? Humility or pride? Was al-Hallaj presuming to be nothing—or everything? Rumi found so much inspiration in al-Hallaj that he included him in his masterpiece and quatrains. To Rumi, al-Hallaj was admitting to the emptiness of his own being—and asserting the total oneness of being—that only God exists.

Don't come to us without the tambourine, for we're feasting!
Get up and play the kettledrums, for I'm Mansur al-Hallaj!
We are drunk, but not drunk from grape wine.
We are so far away from anything you can imagine!

Dervishes who invited public condemnation by seemingly disregarding the outward rites of Islam were called *malamati* (people of reproach), whereas more traditional Muslim mystics were usually simply called Sufis or dervishes. Rumi also occasionally uses the term *qalandar*, which was used for wandering anarchist dervishes who rejected all social norms to be completely free from convention and abide only in the spiritual realm.

O soul, every oppression that comes from you,
is better than faithfulness from other fair ones.
Every blasphemy that manifests in loving you,
comes to be better than belief in the end.

In contrast to Rumi's affection for al-Hallaj, Shams of Tabriz rejected al-Hallaj's pronouncement. In Shams's view, such a bold profession deserved punishment—either through execution or a compelled repentance. Rumi's son supported Rumi's stance, and he mentions al-Hallaj's execution in his own writing, praising him as "sacred and unique."

A HUNDRED DRUMS

A hundred kettledrums are being played in our hearts—
yet we'll hear the song of them tomorrow!

For there's cotton in our ears,
and hair covering our eyes—
our anxieties for the future,
and the seductive whispers of melancholy.

Let's set this cotton alight with the fire of love,
like al-Hallaj and those of the rank of purity did.

Why keep fire and cotton together?
The two are in opposition,
and opposites never survive.

Since the encounter of love is near,
be joyous of presence
for the day of meeting.

For us, death is happiness and encounter.
For you, it is a time of mourning—
flee from this thinking!

Though this world may be our prison,
the abolition of prisons is pure pleasure!

For the one whose prison was so beautiful—
how then will be the court of the one
who adorned the whole world?

Don't look for constancy in this prison—
for here constancy was never constant.

Rumi's son Sultan Walad wrote that those who killed al-Hallaj scattered his ashes on the river. Then, on the surface of the water, they saw his blood form in the words that led to his death—*"Ana al-Haqq"* (I am the Truth)—and felt remorse for their actions. In one story that Sultan Walad narrated, we get a hint for his appreciation of the conceit behind the path of blame. The story is as follows:

A great and rigid ascetic scholar in Tabriz's bazaar came across an Alawi lying down on the earth unconscious. He had vomited, and his face and beard were covered in vomit. Denigrating and cursing him, he spat on him. That very night, the Prophet reproached him because of this attitude saying, "You expect to be from the people of Paradise claiming that you are a good servant of God and a follower of mine. But you saw me in the middle of bazaar covered in puke but yet you did not take me to your home for a good sleep and did not offer me food. Essentially, servants should serve their lords. But you just spat on me." Upon hearing these words, the scholar said to himself: "When did I do this to the Prophet?" The Prophet said immediately (as if he heard what he said to himself):

"Don't you know that my sons are myself, and our children are our liver?" The scholar awoke from this dream in awe and dread. Immediately afterward he sought and found the Alawi. He offered his house to him, bestowed half of his belongings and properties on him, and dedicated himself to being in constant service to him through the rest of his life.[9]

Because one cannot know if a person is intentionally veiling their inner spiritual state by participating in seemingly forbidden conduct and speech, one must not judge others for their ostensible lack of piety, devotion, or adherence to the pillars of Islam and the mystic path. Not only could a troublemaker and rule breaker be a "saint" in hiding, but he may also be a spiritual guide in disguise. However, the world often has little patience for those whose insights transgress the rigid boundaries of religion. As Rumi wrote, "Life involves being hung like a fruit from a tree—that's why you see two hundred people like Hallaj being hung."

HEART-SUFFERING LOVE

For me, there is a friend, a cave,
  and a heart-suffering love.
And you are that friend and cave, O master!
Protect me!

You are Noah, and the spirit.
You are the opener, and the opened.
And to me, you are the renewed heart
at the door of secrets.

You are the light and the banquet—
and the triumph of Mansur al-Hallaj!
And to me, you are the bird of Mount Sinai,
and I am wounded by your beak.

You are the drop and the ocean—
gentle beauty and overpowering majesty.
And to me, you are sugar and poison—
don't torment me anymore!

You are the meditation cell for the sun,
and the heavenly house of Venus.
And to me, you are the meadow of hope—
show me the way, O friend!

You are the daily fast and the Ramadan fast,
and the harvest from begging.
And to me, you are the water and pitcher—
give me water this time!

You are the seed and the snare,
and the wine and the cup.
And to me, you are ripe—
don't leave me raw!

If my body was less hot-spirited,
it would imprison my heart less often.
But you became the way,
so all these words of mine are not in vain.

* * *

The one who passes by my tomb will become drunk,
and if he rests there, he will become drunk for eternity.

When I arrived in Konya for Rumi's "Wedding Night," which takes place every December 17 to commemorate the date of his death, when he finally met his divine beloved, I was amazed to encounter thousands of dervishes from all over the world—Turkey, Iran, India, Brazil, Syria, Mexico, Pakistan, Lebanon, and America—strolling through the streets for this blessed occasion. I was in Sufi heaven. Arriving at Rumi's tomb, after an impromptu session of whirling and music with Sufis from every corner of the earth in a private dervish lodge, I bowed in the direction of its turquoise cylindrical dome, which I'd recently seen in my dreams become unmoored from its foundations and shoot to the sky to whirl in a blinding beam of light.

As I walked across the threshold of Rumi's mausoleum, decorated by Sultan Selim I, the shackles of my imperfections and shortcomings fell to the floor and trailed behind me. Instead of feeling weighed down by broken wings of sorrow, I felt like a phoenix arriving from the Mount Qaf of the soul. With eyes of wonder, I watched as thousands of open and loving hearts from around the globe packed into the enormous three-room mausoleum and sat in complete silence with contemplative and compassionate smiles. As I walked down a tiny aisle through the sea of dervishes, each Sufi smiled and bowed with their hands over their hearts in my direction, as if to say: you are in my heart.

Pulled almost magnetically to the side of Rumi's sarcophagus, which was draped with a large velvet cloth embroidered in gold and topped with an oversized turban, I stood at his side, with my hand over my heart, and bowed forward in his direction—with my right foot covering my left toe in the Mevlevi way. Near his sarcophagus stood the sarcophagus of his scholarly father, Baha al-Din Walad, along with the graves of dozens of Rumi's relatives. Legend has it that when Rumi was buried, his father's tomb "rose and bowed in reverence."

What better ending could there have been for my forty-day retreat—a retreat that had taught me how to walk in the old dervish way of this mystic master, surrender through selfless service, and whirl with ecstatic longing toward love. I had found a wise and loving guide in Baba, who could read the sorrow and secrets of my heart. My dervish brothers had caught me like a net in my despair and kept me from falling. Through daily practice, I had tasted the liberation found in serving others. My mind had been cleansed and soothed by reading Rumi's poetry, reciting the divine names, and playing music. And in whirling I had tasted spiritual states I didn't know were even possible. With gratitude for all the generosity I had been shown and the blessings I had received, I bowed once more in Rumi's direction, and faded back into the serene sea of silent Sufis that swallowed me whole.

INSANITY

◆

To others, the mystic lover may appear unconventional or insane. But to the mystic, being attached to worldly matters and material goods—chained to the ego and thoughts of reputation—is the real insanity! Having set fire to her reputation and attachment to the approval of others, a dervish is free to fall madly in love with the divine, the source of love itself. A mystic who has danced with madness recognizes that the water she was seeking, she has been swimming in for eternity. It is not enough for her just to love—but to love madly.

I've become drunk from longing for those mystic drunks.
I've become ecstatic from the success of that magic spell.
Fed up with reason, I became such a madman—
that love dragged me to the asylum.

In medieval times, Muslim doctors often saw patients who were suffering from "love sickness"—their desire for an unattainable lover driving them to madness. For Rumi, this is the ideal state of the mystic heart—insane with longing for the beloved.

Oh rose garden of my life, take my life,
for without you my life is depressing.
I am in love with the art of madness—
I am fed up with learning and wisdom.

Rumi wrote many poems about mystics driven by spiritual yearning and devotion to the point of appearing crazy. In Rumi's poems, a lovesick mystic is often described as having a yellow, or sallow, face. When he visits a doctor, he is told there is no cure for his sickness.

> *I went to the doctor and said, "Hey, Zein al-Din,*
> *take my pulse and sample my urine."*
> *He said: "Your lust is mixed with insanity."*
> *I said: "For me, how could it be any other way—*
>   *you can keep your damn cure!"*

Is there any cure for the truly lovesick? Rumi writes: "See the whole world ensnared by debauchery, and by wounds that resemble remedies." The world offers our broken and yearning hearts many useless remedies, which in fact hurt rather than heal, when the best medicine of all—is love!

> *I said to the doctor: Prescribe me a cure.*
> *He took my pulse with his esteemed learning,*
> *and said: "What hurts? You should show me."*
> *So I guided his hand to my passionate heart.*

As far back as the eleventh century, Muslim doctors promoted the therapeutic use of music for depression, and prescribed certain musical modes thought to be healing and beneficial for "melancholics." Medieval Muslim doctors treated different kinds of melancholia—including love-madness. In the words of an old Arabic saying: There are many forms of madness (*al-junūn funūn*). Afforded provisions in the endowments of some medieval asylums were singers, musicians, flutists, violinists, cymbalists, and harpists.

THE KING AND THE MADMEN

Today, the king came secretly before the madmen,
and their mad souls began to shout.
The king recognized my voice among the cries,
for my voice was purified from the breath of animality.

The king made a royal gesture toward me:
"One of the madmen has escaped from his chains!"

O king, if I'm crazy, then you are the Solomon of madmen!
O king, you know the intimate secrets of the birds,
and incantations of the genies!
Over this madman, you should recite a spell!

An old man came before the king and said:
"Bind him with chains! For this madman has caused
disturbance and destruction among the devils!"

My king said: "This madman is not bound by any chain,
except for the chain of my curls.
You do not know his character.
He will break thousands of chains and fly to our hand.
He will embody 'to us they shall return,'
for he is a royal falcon."

Music, of course, is not just an artistic bridge to the divine
but also a healing modality. Playing wind instruments and
whirling were Sufi remedies for the sicknesses of the soul. Most
pronounced in these healing melodies was the sound of the
ney, or the reed flute, which was immortalized by Rumi in his
masterpiece as an image of his aching soul and poetic voice.

The wealth of a man's wisdom is madness.
The love-crazed one is a sage man.
Anyone familiar with the heart on the way of pain
is alienated from himself a thousand times.

During medieval times, from Istanbul to Cairo and Fez, musical performances, dance recitals, and theatrical performances were given to soothe and entertain the mentally ill in special wards. When the famous Ottoman traveler Evilya Çelebi visited the twelfth-century Nur an-Din Hospital in Damascus in 1648, he reported that musical concerts were given three times a day for the mental patients. Other medieval sound therapies included running water, bubbling fountains, and the splashing of waterwheels.

No one is aware of that kingly majesty of yours,
until he's gone home without heart or reason.
A crazy person is one who has seen your face,
and then stayed far from you without going mad.

During the guild parades of the imperial Ottoman processions, the wardens of the insane—two hundred keepers of the asylum wards in Istanbul—would follow the entourage of the chief physicians with hundreds of "madmen" in golden and silver chains.

I went to the beloved, my cheeks stained with tears of blood.
Traces of insanity were visible in my eyes and face.
I'd torn off my chains and busted out,
walking instead with the chains of:
  "Be, and it is!" on my feet.

In this performative and exploitative procession, the asylum wardens carried bottles in their hands, from which they gave medicine to the madmen, while others beat or boxed the mentally ill to keep them in order. Some of the mentally ill on parade were naked; others laughed, cried, swore, and attacked their wardens. Evilya Çelebi, who witnessed these events in person, wrote, "If I were to describe all the fits of the madmen and fools on such a day of public procession, I should fill an entire book."

> *Like you, I was once rational and sane.*
> *I was denying all the lovers.*
> *Then I became crazy, drunk, and unruly—*
> *you might think I was like this my whole life.*

Visiting the tombs of saints for healing was another popular tradition from Fez to Istanbul and Baghdad and beyond, and the practice had even been endorsed by the highest echelons of the medical establishment through colonial times. After the British had gained control of the insane asylum of Abbasiyya, outside of Cairo, the director, John Warnock, remarked in his report of 1896, "It seems to be custom to send lunatics to visit the mosque of certain saints." Other traditional healing treatments included aromatic baths with essential oils, cupping, massage, and drinking flower oil—particularly from violets, daffodils, and roses.

OPIUM

> *Intellect ate opium from the palm of love—*
> *now look at intellect's insanity!*

> *Today, both mad love and rational intellect*
> *have become crazy.*

The Oxus which began to flow
out of love for the sea,
has become the sea.
The Oxus has been obliterated!

When it arrived at love,
it saw an ocean of blood.
Intellect sat in the midst of that blood.

Waves of blood crashed over its crown,
turning it from the six directions to the directionless way—
until it lost itself completely,
and became nimble and elegant in love.

While wandering lost in departing,
    it reached a place—
a place where there was no heaven or earth.

When it tried to go forward, it had no feet,
but if it had stood still,
it would have been swindled.

Suddenly, it could see from both sides
—from obliteration and materiality—
an unshakable light.

One banner and a hundred thousand spears!
It became enthralled by that tender light.

Its stuck feet began to run,
flowing in that amazing plain,
yearning to pass beyond—
and be liberated from self

and everything
below.

Two valleys appeared on its path—
one full of fire and the other roses.

A voice said: "Go into the fire,
and find yourself in the rose garden of ease!

But if you enter the rose garden,
you'll find yourself in fire and furnace.

So fly to the heavens like Jesus,
or fall to the depths like Korah."

Flee and seek the sanctuary of the soul's king,
to escape every trap—
that sun of religion and pride of Tabriz,
who's greater than any attribute you can give him!

Rumi also refers in his poetry repeatedly to the classic un-requited love tale of Layla and Majnun (whose name in Arabic means "crazy"). Majnun was driven insane by his all-consuming love for Layla. Rumi saw Majnun as the perfect model of saintly devotion to the beloved. He painted Majnun as the ideal martyr of love, completely unmoored from the rationality of the intel-lect and plunged into the insanity of the mad lover. As Rumi wrote, "O you who are laughing at this story of mine, you have not yet become Majnun—you are still just a scholar!"

My heart wandered far and wide, until it came to the desert.
The path itself became amazed that my heart arrived there.

Although Majnun went in a frenzy to the mountains,
one hundred mountains came to me, the crazy one,
   because of my yearning.

Reason, intellect, and logic have no place in a heart flooded with love. After one's heart has been struck by love, all that exists is love. Majnun was "crazy" with love for his beloved Layla: he was constantly yearning for her unattainable love in ecstasy. The lovelorn looks he and Layla exchanged were adopted as a model for how Sufi masters and their disciples gaze at each other.

I am drunk on you, not wine or opium.
I've become insane—don't seek proper conduct from Majnun!
One hundred great rivers roar from the boiling of your wine,
and the heavens remain astonished by my whirling.

For high-level masters like Rumi and Shams, the intense gaze that they shared was not just a gaze between spiritual companions—but a mutual gaze of annihilated ones into a mirror reflecting the divine.

O you, the whole world is gazing at your beautiful face.
Manly souls are tearing their robes from love of you.
For all the intimates full of mastery,
being crazy for you is better than the intellect
   of any master.

Rumi himself experienced his own touch of madness the first time Shams left Konya to escape the jealousy of Rumi's other disciples and suspicious gossip. Rumi was further plunged into an unmoored state when Shams mysteriously disappeared forever under unusual circumstances. Whether Shams was murdered or returned to Tabriz, we will never know.

In despair over his master's disappearance behind the veil, Rumi spoke in rhyming Persian couplets, prayed until dawn, and performed musical and whirling meditations day and night. He wrote, "I am not a madman, but they call me that. I am not a stranger, but they drive me away."

> *On the path of truth, wisdom and insanity are one.*
> *On the way of love, self and stranger are the same.*
> *To whom the wine-of-being-one-with-you is given, my love,*
> *in her heart: religion, the Ka'ba and idol temple are one.*

Ultimately, for Rumi, insanity was no different from rationality. On the path of truth, such distinctions and dualities collapse and lose all meaning. Perhaps that is the definition, for some, of madness. There is no longer a self and a stranger, or a lover and beloved. To Rumi, in the religion of love, the idol temple of the pagans and the most sacred site of Islam are one and the same. For many Muslims, such a suggestion is not only heresy but pure lunacy. For others, it is the very essence of holiness and wisdom.

> *I became a lunatic, and for a lunatic, sleep is a mistake!*
> *How can a lunatic know where the way to sleep is?*
> *For God never sleeps and is pure from slumber.*
> *Know that the lunatic of God is the bedfellow of God.*

If a dervish has really let the divine reality flood every ounce and fiber of his being, then what need does a mystic have even for sleep? The divine never rests, thus the annihilated dervish transcends the individual needs of the body, such as for nourishment and rest. Rumi dares to write that the lunatic, or fully realized mystic, is the bedfellow of God. That word—"bedfellow"—is the actual word used in this verse, which has previously been translated in other ways to avoid transmitting the full intensity of what he intended to convey. But the verse is clear: the mystic has given up sleep, or the comforts and needs of the world, to rest for eternity in the intimate company of the beloved.

* * *

Love is crazy and we are crazy
about that madman!
The ego is a commander—
but that commander we command!

"Don't worry about Dilara—she's just *majnun*—you know, crazy," wise old Ibrahim said during my retreat about the old Turkish woman who liked to mock me in Turkish in her high-pitched voice.

Ibrahim explained that Dilara always joined the men at prayer time in the front of the mosque. They let her do what she wanted when she wanted, as she was considered to be "touched by God." While in American psychology her behavior would have been deemed psychotic, in the framework of Islamic psychology and mysticism, she was understood to be taken by God, and hence closer to him than the rest of us.

Whenever I looked out from Baba's window at the candle-stick minarets of the mosque, I imagined what it would have been like to have been a patient in the medieval hospital on its grounds, where centuries ago musicians and singers wandered through its seventy rooms serenading the sick. Or to have just been a wandering dervish staying in its adjacent hostel, which housed travelers and wandering dervishes from all over the region and served two meals a day—including pheasant.

In Turkish culture, the difference between a person who is

deli (insane) and a *veli* (saint) has apparently long been a question, as noted in the old expression, "Some said he was *deli*, while others said he was *veli*." Instead of casting her as a threat to be contained and avoided, the Mevlevi dervishes welcomed her with open arms.

"Can I please have a few dollars to take the bus to Medina?" Dilara said one day, holding out her hand.

The men all laughed at the absurdity of her request, since a bus ride from Istanbul to Medina in Saudi Arabia would certainly be more than several dollars.

"I don't know why you are all laughing," Dilara said. "The bus is just five dollars to Medina."

After several minutes of affectionately mocking her, the men finally realized that the bus from Mecca to Medina—not Istanbul to Medina—was only five dollars. In her mind, you see, she wasn't in Istanbul—she was in Mecca. She was always in Mecca, always on pilgrimage. Maybe she wasn't so crazy after all.

LONGING FOR WATER

You're so thirsty you're acting drunk—
but the water's right in front of you!
You're standing in the water,
unaware of the powerful current!

You're like a pearl in the sea asking:
"Where's the water?"
Your imagination, like the shell of a pearl,
blocks your way to the sea.

Your very question of "Where is it?" is a veil,
like a cloud covering the sun.

The wickedness of your eye
blinds your inner vision—
which is designed to remove
the veil of ignorance
blocking your sight!

And the cotton plugged in your ears has become
the unsound source of your knowledge.

You should align your consciousness with truth—
if you thirst to be his bewildered beloved.

* * *

When your "I" becomes negated from existence,
then what remains?
Think! What remains?

Before I left for America, Baba said he had a surprise for me. He gathered all of his dervishes together and told me to sit next to him on his long floor cushion. Set before me was a large, round black music case. I hurriedly unlocked it and discovered a brand new set of kettledrums inside. Next to the drums was a first-class *ney*, which Baba said I should practice every day.

"Without your realizing it, I have been working on you on multiple levels this entire time; without knowing it, a dervish is painted by the color of the shaykh. You will not see the fruits of my labor until you return home," he said.

After a month away from so-called real life, I really didn't want to return to my daily life of working and paying bills. Why couldn't I just live a spiritual life, free from all the trappings of materiality, I wondered.

I was well aware that the Sufi way is not a path of retreat from the world, but a way of seeking transcendence while still actively present in it. Engagement in the world does provide opportunities for spiritual growth—to practice love, compassion, awareness, generosity, and nonattachment—but I was unconvinced. I wanted to live in a hollowed-out tree in the forest, or a cave in the desert—far away from injustices and cruelties of humanity.

As I took out the sticks and tested out my new kettledrums, Baba detected the brewing conflict and anxiety rising in my mind and heart. He could tell that I was hesitant to reenter my worldly realm in America.

Peering into my eyes, he leaned forward.

"Listen: life is like a bird with two wings," he said. "One wing is the material world—money and daily-life concerns—the other wing is love, ecstasy, and meditative bliss. To fly, we need both."

A NEW MADNESS

Today, a new madness has arrived.
It has dragged the chains
of a thousand hearts.

Today, it has torn open the sides
of the white sugar bags.

Again, the bedouin has bought
that Joseph of beauty
for eighteen counterfeit coins.

All night long, souls in glory and grace
grazed on daffodils and jasmine,

until dawn when every soul
nimbly and elegantly leapt up.

Today, the violet bed and tulips
  have blossomed
from stones and clods.
The trees have bloomed in winter.
In January, fruits have ripened.

You could say God has created
  a new world
in this worn-out world.

O gnostic, O lover, recite this poem,
for love has chosen you from all the lovers.

On your golden cheek there's a bite mark—
has that silvery-breasted beloved bitten you?

He should cherish the heart that's throbbed
so much in longing for him.

Now hush, and go stroll through the meadow—
for today our eyes will behold the succession.

NOTES

◆

1. "They say that I am a saint. I said, 'OK, 'let it be so, but what happiness does it bring to me?' If I were to be proud of it, it would be very ugly; but Mevlana [Rumi], if one looks at the attributes defined by the Qur'an and the sayings of the Prophet, is a saint. And I am the saint of the saint, the friend of the friend; therefore I am less easily shaken, more firm."

   Selections from *The Conversations* (Maqalat) *of Shams of Tabriz,* https://sufism.org/sufism/writings-on-sufism/the-conversations -maqalat-of-shams-of-tabriz-2.

2. "Why don't our friends take pleasure in that clean and infinite universe of ours? This universe embraces them and makes them drunk without ever making them aware of it. Everyone is in unanimous agreement that this universe is not a forbidden substance. Whereas wine is forbidden."

   Selections from *The Conversations* (Maqalat) *of Shams of Tabriz,* https://sufism.org/sufism/writings-on-sufism/the-conversations -maqalat-of-shams-of-tabriz-2.

3. "He is the kind of person before whom human beings and angels put their ladders down in admiration of his qualities and words. Acrobats who astonish people with their rope skills are amazed at the length and strength of his rope, and by the fearlessness and heroism of his feats. Hearts leap at the sight of his miracles."

   Selections from *The Conversations* (Maqalat) *of Shams of Tabriz,* https://sufism.org/sufism/writings-on-sufism/the-conversations -maqalat-of-shams-of-tabriz-2.

4. "It is blasphemy to say that the *Sema* performed by God's people is a sin. That hand which moves without the Divine exuberance will burn in hell for sure, and the hands that rise in *Sema* will reach paradise—for sure."

   Selections from *The Conversations* (Maqalat) *of Shams of Tabriz*, https://sufism.org/sufism/writings-on-sufism/the-conversations -maqalat-of-shams-of-tabriz-2.

5. "The shayk said, 'The Caliph has forbidden the *Sema*.' This prohibition turned into a knot within a certain dervish. He fell ill and they took him to a specialist. He examined his pulse and looked for the cause of illness. It was like nothing he had ever learned about. He couldn't find anything wrong with him, but the dervish died. Afterwards, the doctor performed an autopsy and found the knot within his chest. It had become a carnelian. The doctor kept this gem until a time when he needed some extra cash. The gem passed from hand to hand until it reached the caliph, who had the gem set into a ring. One day, that same caliph was attending a *Sema*, watching from above, when he discovered that his clothes were covered with blood. He examined himself but could find no wound anywhere. He felt for his ring and the stone was gone. Later they traced that gem back to its original owner and the doctor told them the whole story mentioned above."

   Shams of Tabriz, from the *Maqalat of Shams-i-Tabriz* as quoted in *The Knowing Heart: A Sufi Path of Transformation* by Kabir Helminski and https://sufism.org/origins/mevlevi/*sema* /the-gate-of-secrets-by-kabir-helminski-2.

6. "One day Mowlana [Rumi] came to Plato's Monastery which stands at the foot of a mountain, and he went into the cave from which cold water flows forth. He set off to penetrate to the very end of the cave. I waited outside the cave watching to see what would happen. Mowlana [Rumi] sat in the middle of the cold water for seven days and nights. After that, filled with passionate excitement, he came outside and departed. Truly, there was no trace of change whatsoever in his blessed body."

The monk watched in astonishment as Rumi performed the miraculous feat of meditating for seven days in cold water. The monk also swore that: "What I have read about the person of the Messiah and in the sacred books of Abraham and Moses, as well as what I have seen in the histories of the ancestors concerning the magnitude of the austerities of the prophets—the very same, and even more, was in Mowlana [Rumi]."

The Feats of the Knowers of God: Manāqeb Al-'ārefīn, by Shams al-Dīn Aḥmad Aflākī, Shams al-Dīn Aḥmad. *The Feats of the Knowers of God: Manāqeb Al-'ārefīn.* O'Kane, John (translator). Leiden: Brill, 2002.

7. "Whoso questions the truth of this—whosoever is unconvinced by the proof—let him engage in mystical disciplines and service to those visionaries, that perchance he will, as one dazzled by the thunderbolt, see the light blazing in the Kingdom of Power and will witness the heavenly essences and lights that Hermes and Plato beheld. He will see the spiritual luminaries, the wellsprings of kingly splendor and wisdom that Zoroaster told of, and that which the good and blessed king Kay-Khosraw unexpectedly beheld in a flash. All the sages of Persia were agreed thereon. . . . These are the lights to which Empedocles and others alluded."

From "Plato to the Shāhnāma: Reflections on Saintly Veneration in Seljuk Konya," *Sacred Spaces and Urban Networks*, ed. S. Yalman and A. H. Uğurlu (Istanbul: ANAMED, 2019), 119–40. Suzan Yalman, https://www.academia.edu/41177347/_From _Plato_to_the_Sh%C4%81hn%C4%81ma_Reflections_on _Saintly_Veneration_in_Seljuk_Konya.

8. "How can you deliver a secret belonging to the high to the low? Can a bird that has fallen into a trap fly? Can an old woman fight like a brave champion? Those who are veiled from God cannot reach the station of possessing spiritual states and words. Those mystical states and words belong to the King. Who can be privy to that secret by struggling and striving for his lower soul? Food meant for a falcon will cause a small bird to suffocate and choke.

One should accept little as much. One should be content with a pitcher rather than the sea."

Küçük, Hülya. "Sulṭān Walad's Role in the Foundation of the Mevlevi Sufi Order." *Mawlana Rumi Review*, vol. 3 (2012), pp. 22–50. Leiden: Brill. https://www.jstor.org/stable/45236331.

9. "A great and rigid ascetic scholar in Tabriz's bazaar came across an Alawi lying down on the earth unconscious. He had vomited, and his face and beard were covered in vomit. Denigrating and cursing him, he spat on him. That very night, the Prophet reproached him because of this attitude saying, 'You expect to be from the people of Paradise claiming that you are a good servant of God and a follower of mine. But you saw me in the middle of bazaar covered in puke but yet you did not take me to your home for a good sleep and did not offer me food. Essentially, servants should serve their lords. But you just spat on me.' Upon hearing these words, the scholar said to himself: 'When did I do this to the Prophet?' The Prophet said immediately (as if he heard what he said to himself): 'Don't you know that my sons are myself, and our children are our liver?' The scholar awoke from this dream in awe and dread. Immediately afterwards he sought and found the Alawi. He offered his house to him, bestowed half of his belongings and properties on him, and dedicated himself to being in constant service to him through the rest of his life."

Küçük, Hülya. "Sulṭān Walad's Role in the Foundation of the Mevlevi Sufi Order." *Mawlana Rumi Review*, vol. 3 (2012), pp. 22–50. Leiden: Brill. https://www.jstor.org/stable/45236331.

BIBLIOGRAPHY

◆

Aflākī, Shams al-Dīn Aḥmad. *The Feats of the Knowers of God: Manāqeb Al-ʿārefîn*. O'Kane, John (translator). Leiden: Brill, 2002.

Arberry, A. J. *Discourses of Rumi*. Oxfordshire: Routledge; 1st edition, June 2, 2004.

Attar, Sholeh Wolpé (translator). *The Conference of the Birds*. W. W. Norton & Company; Reprint edition, March 7, 2017.

Blann, Gregory, and Fariha al-Jerrahi (postscript). *Lifting the Boundaries: Muzaffer Efendi and the Transmission of Sufism to the West*. New York: Pir Press, 2016.

Chittick, William C. *Divine Love: Islamic Literature and the Path to God*. New Haven: Yale University Press, 2013.

———. *Ibn ʿArabi: Heir to the Prophets*. Oxford: Oneworld, 2005.

———. *The Sufi Doctrine of Rumi*. World Wisdom Books, June 16, 2005.

———. *The Sufi Path of Love: The Spiritual Teachings of Rumi*. Albany: State University of New York Press, 1983.

———. *Sufism: A Beginner's Guide*. Oxford: Oneworld Publications, October 1, 2007.

———. *Sufism: A Short Introduction*. Oxford: Oneworld Publications, 2000.

Douglas-Klotz, Neil. *The Sufi Book of Life: 99 Pathways of the Heart for the Modern Dervish*. London: Penguin Books. February 22, 2005.

Ernst, Carl W. *Refractions of Islam in India: Situating Sufism and Yoga*. Thousand Oaks: Sage Publications Pvt. Ltd, June 20, 2016.

————. *Sufism: An Introduction to the Mystical Tradition of Islam.* Boulder: Shambhala, May 10, 2011.

———— (translator). *Hallaj: Poems of a Sufi Martyr* (author: Husayn ibn Mansur Hallaj). Evanston: Northwestern University Press, July 15, 2018.

Frager, Robert (editor), and James Fadiman (editor). *Essential Sufism.* HarperOne; Reprint edition, November 17, 1999.

Gooch, Brad. *Rumi's Secret.* New York: Harper, 2017.

Hansen, Valerie. *The Silk Road: A New History.* Oxford: Oxford University Press, 2012.

Harvey, Andrew. *The Way of Passion: A Celebration of Rumi.* Berkeley: Frog, Ltd. 1994.

Helminski, Camille Adams. *Women of Sufism: A Hidden Treasure.* Boulder: Shambhala Publications, February 25, 2003.

Helminski, Kabir. *Holistic Islam: Sufism, Transformation, and the Needs of Our Time* (Islamic Encounter Series). Ashland: White Cloud Press, September 1, 2017.

————. *In the House of Remembering: The Living Tradition of Sufi Teaching.* Brattleboro: Threshold Books, September 29, 2020.

————. *The Knowing Heart: A Sufi Path of Transformation.* Boulder: Shambhala Publications, October 24, 2000.

————. *Living Presence (revised): The Sufi Path to Mindfulness and the Essential Self.* New York: TarcherPerigee, May 30, 2017.

Hirtenstein, Stephen. *The Unlimited Mercifier: The Spiritual Life and Thought of Ibn Arabi.* Ashland, Oregon: Anqa Publishing, 1999.

Hirtenstein, Stephen (translator), and Ibn Arabi. *The Four Pillars of Spiritual Transformation: The Adornment of the Spiritually Transformed.* Anqa Publishing, June 1, 2009.

al-Jerrahi, Shayka Fatima Fariha. *Invitation to Union.* New York: Pir Press, January 1, 1999.

al-Jerrahi Al-Halveti, Tosun Bayrak (photographer), and Shems Friedlander (designer). *The Most Beautiful Names.* Threshold Books, November 1, 1983.

Karamustafa, Ahmet T. *Sufism: The Formative Period*. Berkeley and Los Angeles: University of California Press, 2007.

Knysh, Alexander. *Sufism: A New History of Islamic Mysticism*. Princeton: Princeton University Press, October 31, 2017.

Küçük, Hülya. "Sulṭān Walad's Role in the Foundation of the Mevlevi Sufi Order." *Mawlana Rumi Review*, vol. 3 (2012), pp. 22–50. Leiden: Brill. https://www.jstor.org/stable/45236331.

Lewis, Franklin D. *Rumi: Past and Present, East and West*. Oxford: A Oneworld Book, 2008, revised paperback edition. First published in hardback by Oneworld Publications, 2005.

Lewisohn, Leonard. *The Heritage of Sufism: Classical Persian Sufism from Its Origins to Rumi* (700–1300), vol. 1. Oneworld Publications (April 30, 2018) / World Wisdom (January 30, 2015).

———. *The Philosophy of Ecstasy: Rumi and the Sufi Tradition*. World Wisdom: The Library of Perennial Philosophy / Spiritual Masters: East & West.

Mojaddedi, Jawid. (Translator and Jalal al-Din Rumi is the author). *The Masnavi* (Books 1–4), Oxford World's Classics, October 15, 2008.

Reinhertz, Shakina. *Women Called to the Path of Rumi: The Way of the Whirling Dervish*. Hohm Press, February 25, 2015.

Rumi. *Masnavi-ye Ma'navi*, ed., R. A. Nicholson as *The Mathnawi of Jalalu'ddin Rumi*, E. J. W. Gibb Memorial, new series. London: Luzac & Co., 1925, 1929, 1933.

Rumi (author), Nesreen Akhtarkhavari (translator), and Anthony A. Lee (translator). *Love Is My Savior: The Arabic Poems of Rumi*. East Lansing: Michigan State University Press, February 1, 2016.

Rumi, Jalal al-Din (author), Ehsan Yarshater (editor), Franklin D. Lewis (foreword), and A. J. Arberry (translator). *Mystical Poems of Rumi*. Chicago: University of Chicago Press, April 15, 2009.

Safi, Omid. *The Politics of Knowledge in Premodern Islam: Negotiating Ideology and Religious Inquiry*. Chapel Hill: University of North Carolina Press, 2006.

Sargut, Cemalnur. *Beauty and Light: Mystical Discourses by a Contemporary Female Sufi Master.* Louisville: Fons Vitae, July 1, 2018.

Sargut, Cemalnur, Bruce B. Lawrence, Dilek Güldütuna, Emine Yeniterzi, James Morris, Kabir Helminski, miriam cooke, Mohammed Rustom, Omid Safi, and William C. Chittick. *Rumi's Love of the Prophet.* Nefes Publishing, February 1, 2021.

Schimmel, Annemarie. *As Through a Veil: Mystical Poetry in Islam.* Oxford: Oneworld Publications, 2001, originally published 1982.

———. *Mystical Dimensions of Islam.* Chapel Hill: University of North Carolina Press, 1975.

———. *Rumi's World: The Life and Work of the Great Sufi Poet.* Boston & London: Shambhala Press, 2001; originally published as *I Am Wind, You Are Fire.*

———. *The Triumphal Sun.* Albany: State University of New York Press, 1993.

Sedgwick, Mark. *Sufism: The Essentials.* Cairo: The American University in Cairo Press, September 1, 2003.

———. *Western Sufism: From the Abbasids to the New Age.* Oxford: Oxford University Press, October 18, 2016.

Sells, Michael. *Approaching the Qur'an: The Early Revelations.* Ashland: White Cloud Press, January 1, 1999.

Shams of Tabriz. Selections from *The Conversations* (Maqalat) *of Shams of Tabriz,* https://sufism.org/sufism/writings-on-sufism/the-conversations-maqalat-of-shams-of-tabriz-2.

Shams of Tabriz (author), Camille Helminski (translator), and Refik Algan (translator). *Rumi's Sun: The Teachings of Shams of Tabriz.* Brattleboro: Threshold Books, November 26, 2015.

Yalman, S., and A. H. Uğurlu, eds. "From Plato to the Shāhnāma: Reflections on Saintly Veneration in Seljuk Konya," *Sacred Spaces and Urban Networks* (Istanbul: ANAMED, 2019), 119–40. https://www.academia.edu/41177347/_From_Plato_to_the_Sh%C4%81hn%C4%81ma_Reflections_on_Saintly_Veneration_in_Seljuk_Konya_.

Zargar, Cyrus Ali. *Polished Mirror: Storytelling and the Pursuit of Virtue in Islamic Philosophy and Sufism*. Oxford: Oneworld Academic, November 2, 2017.

Zarrinkub, A. H. *Step by Step Up to Union with God: Life, Thought and Spiritual Journey of Jalal-al-Din Rumi*, trans. by M. Kayvani. New York: Persian Heritage Foundation, 2009.

ACKNOWLEDGMENTS

◆

This book breathes only because of the kindness, support, and generosity of a loving caravan of compassionate hearts around the globe. Islamic mysticism is a living tradition and vast ocean. Everywhere I have wandered for the past two decades—along the Silk Road through sixty countries, from Indonesia to Mali and many places in between—I have been welcomed by the open hearts and helping hands of Muslim mystics. I have learned at the feet of living saints and had my own life transformed and even saved on more than one occasion by the heroic efforts and nourishing wisdom of mystic masters and their exceptional disciples. Their spiritual guidance, boundless generosity, and astonishing humility have sustained and inspired me. Had I not been blessed by their mystic knowledge, exemplary compassion, and loving kindness, I would have been lost.

I wish to express my heartfelt gratitude first to my Persian language teachers at Brown University, Harvard University, and the American Institute of Persian Studies in Tajikistan for giving me a solid foundation in the art of translation to understand Persian poetry and read Rumi in the original. In particular, I would like to thank Dr. Maryam Shariati, Homeira Niavarani, and Dr. Dalia Yasharpour, for guiding me through the intricacies of Persian grammar and educating me in the profound richness of Persian literature, history, and culture.

I was able to read and translate Rumi's Arabic poetry thanks to having studied for so many years with Mirena Christoff, my amazing Arabic professor at Brown University. My colleague and friend Dr. David Wilmsen was also very generous in offering feedback on my translations of Rumi's Arabic poetry and other Arabic-related matters.

I am eternally indebted to Nougeanne Kumaily for so generously helping me to translate the more difficult passages of *The Masnavi*, and for sharing his extraordinary expertise in excavating the nuances of certain principles, allusions, and terms. I treasure all that I learned from him as we dove into exploring and contemplating the deeper meanings of Rumi's verses together. Likewise, the profound insights and generous spirit of my wise friend Hadi Khalili Shavarini were instrumental in helping me to "pierce the pearl" of Rumi's poetry, and I thank him for his astounding patience, as I obsessed over and dissected every word. Our shared journey into Rumi's beautiful heart has been such a sweet blessing! A special note of thanks, too, to his brother, Mehdi Khalili Shavarini, for illuminating us on the mystical meanings of certain verses, and for our lovely time together in Tehran. I also appreciate the assistance of Dr. Omid Safi, Dr. Behnaz Mirzai, Dr. Nahid Siamdoust, Ilyas al-Kashani and Dr. Alireza Korangy in helping me define some difficult words and refine various verses.

This book never would have been born without the invaluable encouragement, unconditional support, and insightful wisdom of my agent, Jacqueline Flynn at Joelle Delbourgo Associates Literary Agency, who was pivotal in its conception and completion. Likewise, I am touched by and grateful for the extraordinary openness, compassion, and courage of Joel Fotinos in publishing this book, and much beholden to the dedicated and impressive efforts of associate editor Gwen Hawkes and copyeditor Kate Davis in bringing it to fruition with such precision, attention, and care. Thanks as well to talented photographer Eddie Chu and to Jen Hadley and Emily Gordon for photo processing help.

For the opportunity to dive further into Persian and Sufism as a postdoctoral fellow at Harvard, I must acknowledge with gratitude Professor Homi Bhabha, the Mahindra Humanities Center at Harvard University, and the Department of Near Eastern Languages and Civilizations at Harvard. My knowledge in Islamic law was further enhanced by my time at Harvard as a research fellow on the Islamopedia Initiative and an editor of SHARIASource and by my position at Yale Law School as a Research Scholar in Law and Islamic Law and Civilization Research Fellow in the Abdallah S. Kamel Center for the Study of Islamic Law and Civilization.

I am much obliged to those who have supported and encouraged my Persian-related scholarship, especially Dr. Ali Gheissari, Dr. Lawrence Potter, Dr. Abbas Amanat, Dr. Janet Afari, Dr. Alborz Ghandehari, Dr. Nader El-Bizri, Dr. Kristian Petersen, and Dr. Maher Jarrar. Thank you as well to Brad Gooch for his stellar and informative biography of Rumi.

A number of fellowships helped deepen my understanding of Islam, Islamic law, and Islamic mysticism and gave me the opportunity to learn directly from mystic guides while visiting countless Sufi shrines across the Islamic world: the Edward A. Hewett Policy Fellowship (Tajikistan and Afghanistan), Fulbright-Hays Fellowship (Indonesia), Harvard Traveling Fellowship (Iran), Columbia Pepsico Fellowship (Uzbekistan), IREX Fellowship (Kazakhstan, Kyrgyzstan, Czech & Slovak Republics), American Center for Mongolian Studies Fellowship (Mongolia), American Center for Indonesian Studies Fellowship (Indonesia), American Councils Fellowship (Turkmenistan), American University of Beirut Travel Grant (Mongolia), and State Department Critical Language Fellowship (Tajikistan). My graduate studies in the Harriman Institute at Columbia University were also essential to my understanding of history, politics, and cultures on the Silk Road.

I have nothing but the most amazing memories from my trips to the Islamic Republic of Iran, and I would like to thank Harvard University, Sharif University, and the Commonwealth Club of California for making these travels possible. Special thanks as well to Dr. Ali Meghdari and Ms. Narjes Shafiee for their kind and enlightening hospitality on my first trip to Iran, and to all those who made it possible for me to speak at Tehran University and Sharif University. To my dear brother Ali Sadrnia, the best guide in Iran, thank you for all you have taught me on our very special adventures through Iran's cultural heritage sites, architectural masterpieces, and glorious history—I will look back on our travels together fondly and with much happiness and nostalgia for the rest of my life.

There are too many mystic masters to thank by name; however, I must acknowledge my indebtedness to the enlightened guidance, gnostic knowledge, and boundless love of Shaykha Fariha al-Jerrahi, Haje Hayat, Cemalnur Sargut, Dr. Malik Badri, Dr. Ibrahim Farajaje, Haci Yakub Baba, Hüseyin Dede, Edip Baba, Soufi Adama, and Dr. Kamal Samhoun. Blessings upon them all!

Were I to name all the beautiful mystic hearts in Sudan, Iran, Algeria, Morocco, Mali, Ethiopia, Palestine, Indonesia, India, Malaysia, Russia, Turkey, Oman, Tunisia, Tanzania, Jordan, Egypt, Syria, Lebanon, Afghanistan, China, Karakalpakstan, Tajikistan, Turkmenistan, Uzbekistan, Kyrgyzstan, the Czech Republic, Hungary, Mongolia, and the United States who shepherded me on my journeys, their names would fill an entire book. I extend my deepest gratitude and best wishes to them all.

In particular, I wish to thank the following kind souls for

making my far-reaching journeys so soul-enriching and life-changing: Dr. Nasir Raza Khan, Dr. Khaled Tadmori, Dr. Professor Abdeldjallil Youcef Larbi, Yunus Irmak, Hüseyin Gökhan Çalışkan, Kemal Sağlam, Hüseyin Bayazıt, the Muftiate of Istanbul, Sirojiddin Juraev, Dr. Amna Badri, Dr. Peter Dorman, Dr. Martha Joukwsky, Dr. Stéphanie Melyon-Reinette, Dr. Barbara Drieskens, Dina Habbal, Lena Lahham, Souha Nasreddine, Abed Samhuri, Sirojiddin Juraev, Ameen Alkutainy, Dr. Carter Johnson, Gulya Bekniyazova, Gulbahar Abdurasulova, Dr. Demberel Sukhbaatar, Dr. Peter Hessler, Leslie Chang, Dr. Tony Ho, Claudia Cooper, Jackie Lamb, Dr. James McDougall, David Jeffrey, Angela Lankford, Dr. James Garrett, Courtland Cox, Seydou Coulibaly, Dr. Michael Antonucci, Peter Sellars, Isma'il Kushkush, Getachew Mengistu, Dr. Walid Bouchakour, Dr. Asad Ali, Nuha al-Abed, Bilel Fasla, Abdunasir A. Garad, Penelope Mitchell, Bekhzod Shatulyaganov, Shukhrat Tashkhojaev, Hrag Vosgerichian, Fatma Al Mamari, Omaima Al Hinai, Brian Wood, Jane and David Posnett, Meriel Carboni, Mary Beth San Juan (Reyhan), Jean Said Makdisi, Abram Iskhakov, Dr. Mariam Ayad, Dr. Abbas El Siddik, Dr. Malik Muhammad Hafeez, Sheikh Abdul Khaleel, Ayatullah Rajabov, Marina Parisinou, Kate Bornstein, Marston Luce, Deborah de Gorter Martin, Udval Shijirbaatar, Dolgorsuren Galaa, Manos, my tai chi masters and friends in China, Abdulhafiz and his Sufi dig crew in Sudan, the Dervish Brothers Center of Konya, my Uyghur guide in East Turkestan, and my Afghan host family. And, of course, all the drivers!

I was very fortunate to study whirling in Egypt with my teacher Muhammad, in America with Hafizullah Chishti, and in Turkey with dear Baba, as well as to meet helpful companions and guides along the way, like my fellow Mevlevi-Slavic-Chihuahua-loving sister Natasha Alexiouk, Paul Raushenbush,

Halil Baba, John McGeehan, Judith Wood, Nafisa Degani, Marilyn Perez, Mustafa Farhad, Ameena Meer, Nancy Barta-Norton (Lakshmi), Joseph Norton (Muhasibi), Aziza Scott, Pir Zia Inayat Khan, Kabir Helminski, Dr. William Chittick, and Dr. Sachiko Murata.

During my monthlong retreat in Istanbul, I received loving support, witty companionship, and much-needed comic relief from Dr. Logan Sparks, the enduring mirror of my heart. The theological brilliance of Dr. Rev. Yorke Peeler, the courageous compassion of Dr. Rev. Betty Bailey, and the pastoral brilliance and loving friendship of Rev. Janet Cooper-Nelson have also provided spiritual inspiration and comfort for my soul.

Having faced many obstacles on the path to finishing this book—from a medical emergency while yak herding with Tibetan nomads fourteen thousand feet up in the Himalayas of Tibet to a ridiculous interrogation by the Chinese Communist Party for bearing witness to their crimes against humanity in occupied Tibet—I would not have managed to bring this book to completion without the loving encouragement, essential feedback, and unwavering support of the man with a heart of gold and mind of a genius, Isaac Hurwitz, and the life-sustaining wisdom, heart-expanding friendship, and righteous consciousness of my beloved soul sister, Dr. Jasmine Syedullah. All of my endeavors and journeys—be they on the intellectual plane, in cultures far from my own, or in that bewildering realm of the heart—have been guided by the incomparable wisdom, abiding love, and good humor of Dr. John Emigh, my soul's captain, whose mentorship has shaped my life and this book.

From exploring Borobudur in Java to brunching in Beirut and avoiding sharks at Treasure Beach in Jamaica, I've learned so much alongside my adventurous mate and popcorn guru, Dr. Kimberly Clair, and I'm very grateful to her and her husband, David Clair (along with Penari), for giving me a sense of "home." I'm also thankful for the always dependable and generous help of Carol Collins, the longtime custodian of my heart's secrets, as well as the support and friendship of Dr. Kamala Russell, Bob and Annie Wait, Mary Halpenny-Kilip, Dr. Michael Vermy, Dr. Brigitte Treumann, Dr. Alice Slotsky, Jody Milano, Dr. David Konstan, Ivana Husakova, Shana Harvey, Manya Rubinstein, Clay Rockefeller, Ullie Emigh, Michelle Bach-Coulibaly, Lorraine Paterson, Teresa Wells, Junius Williams, Marianne Barcellona, Bo, John K., Judy Marcus, Barbara Brookes, Mollie Glick, Dr. Mitra Shavarini, Dr. Maryam Saleh, Normal Snapp, Thomas Lane, and Dr. Masako Fidler.

The mystical music my Javanese gamelan gang and I have made together, the shadow puppets we have accompanied, and the countless laughs we have shared have woven such joy and beauty into the tapestry of my life: thank you, Anne Stebinger, Leslie Rudden, Carla Scheele, I. M. Harjito, Dr. Marc Perlman, Mas Darsono, and Harold Augenbraum, for always supporting and nurturing me. Thanks also to my rock-climbing partners, Jeannine Peterson and Dru Hartley, for literally holding my life in your hands on our gravity-defying adventures in nature and helping me realize the full extent of my endurance, power, and strength.

The experimental masterpieces and commitment to craft of the writers with whom I studied and worked at Brown University inevitably influenced my writing, and I'm grateful for their groundbreaking creative work and guidance: Aishah Rahman, Paula Vogel, Nilo Cruz, Charles Mee, Keith and Rosemarie Waldrop, C. D. Wright, Forrest Gander, Gale Nelson, Brian Evenson, Robert Coover, Thalia Field, Ben Lerner, and Carol Maso.

It takes a village to keep me well and thriving. Thank you

to Fran Rasmussen and Dr. Steve Rasmussen for rescuing me from myself and setting me on the Sufi path, to Dr. Alison Heru for being the guardian angel watching over me, and to Dr. Ellen Nasper for heroically going above and beyond the call of duty to help me survive the pandemic in China, heal from illness in Tibet, and radically transform my consciousness. You are all miracle workers of the highest order.

I'm fortunate to have had such a compassionate and talented group of healers and confidants, and their expertise and generosity have significantly improved the quality of my life: Dr. Mary Cox, Deborah Silverstein, Lenora Briggs, Dr. Kay Redfield Jamison, Pat Faiola, Dr. Anil Ranawat, Dr. Diren Arsoy, Dr. Erica Spatz, Dr. Peter Byers, Dr. John Pappas, Dr. Paul Fortgang, Dr. Elizabeth Richey, Dr. Ali Abadi, Dr. Edouardo Yoshida, Dr. Rashid Hussain, Dr. Nwanmegha Young, Dr. Alfred Lavi, Dr. Ghassan Kanazi, Dr. Fadila Naji, Dr. Brandon Qualls, Dr. Alan Hakim, Dr. Brad Tinkle, Dr. Jeanne Catanzaro, Dr. Karen Weiss, Lara Bloom, Jocelyn Sherman, Judith Braden, S. Black, and Jackie Santana.

My adventurous mother was the first to nurture in me a love of poetry and encourage my spiritual seeking and far-flung travels. I will forever cherish our blessed time together in Rumi's majestic mausoleum in Konya on his "Wedding Night," our ecstasy in gazing down upon whirling dervishes in a Sufi lodge in Istanbul, and our retreat in the breathtaking Sufi shrine of Ahmed al-Tijani in Fez on Eid al-Adha, as well as our wanderings through countless mosques, mystic shrines, and sacred landscapes in Egypt, Morocco, Lebanon, Kenya, Zanzibar, and the Sultanate of Oman. Thank you to my brother, too, for often coming along for the ride.

It was from my generous grandmother that I learned the sweet pleasure of being spoiled by love and from my compassionate grandfather the true meaning of unconditional love (not to mention Slavic pride and comic timing). Thank you, too, to my uncle, aunt, great-aunt, and cousin for teaching me the overwhelming power and enduring beauty of love, and to my birth mother who gave me the best Slavic name of all: Sasha. Blessings on the first human hands that ever held me and ushered me into this existence—those of Dr. Sheikh.

My greatest teachers in love (forgive me for the heresy) have been my Chihuahua companions, who have opened and expanded my heart more than I ever thought possible. Anubis Ramses, Abutiu Khufu, Samson, and Delilah, I love you all so much. I am also grateful to all those who helped care for them, especially Dr. Petar Bogunovic, Dr. Lisa MacKay, Andrea Whaibe, Kathy Briggs, Patty Burns, Zoe Keller, Susan Levy, and Anubis's acupuncturist and Abu's vets in China.

Teaching Persian poetry and Sufism to college students in Lebanon, Oman, and China showed me the universal appeal of mysticism and the essential truths of Rumi's verses. When I taught a course at Columbia University on Sufism, my students said they were drawn to taking the course because they had never heard anything about Islamic mysticism. It is my sincere hope that this book has served, in some small way, as an introduction to the mystical concepts at the core of Rumi's poems. I hope you will forgive me for any translation mistakes I have inadvertently made or information I have left out. Apologies as well for anyone I forgot to include.

And, finally, to my eternal beloved—who makes every atom of my being pulse with praise and sing out in gratitude—that lifegiving light, who goes by many names and first ignited in me the fire of love: an ocean of love, most of all, to you, my love, the true master of my heart.

ABOUT THE AUTHOR

◆

Eddie Chu

Dr. Emily Jane O'Dell is an associate professor at Sichuan University–Pittsburgh Institute in China. She has served as the Whittlesey Chair of History and Archaeology at the American University of Beirut, an assistant professor at Sultan Qaboos University in Oman, a Research Scholar in Law and Islamic Law and Civilization Research Fellow at Yale Law School, and an editor for Harvard Law School's SHARIASource, an online portal. Stateside she has taught at Columbia, Brown, and Harvard, where she received an award for teaching excellence. Her research can be found in *Iranian Studies, International Journal of Persian Literature, Journal of Global Slavery, Journal of Africana Religions, Obsidian: Literature & Arts in the African Diaspora, Journal of Literary and Cultural Disability Studies, Disability & Society,* and SHARIASource. Her writing has appeared in *The New York Times, Al Jazeera,* NPR, *The Louisville Review, Counter-Punch, Salon, TRT World, The Christian Science Monitor,* and *HuffPost.*